Music of the NEW AMERICAN NATION

Sacred Music
from 1780 to 1820

KARL KROEGER, GENERAL EDITOR
University of Colorado at Boulder

Contents of the Series

VOLUME 11

Samuel Babcock (ca. 1760–1813)

The Collected Works

Edited by
LAURIE J. SAMPSEL

Routledge
Taylor & Francis Group
NEW YORK AND LONDON

First published 1999 by Garland Publishing, Inc.

This edition published 2013 by Routledge
605 Third Avenue, New York, NY 10017
2 Park Square, Milton Park, Abingdon, Oxon OX14 4RN

Routledge is an imprint of the Taylor & Francis Group, an informa business

Library of Congress Cataloging-in-Publication Data

Samuel Babcock (ca. 1760–1813) : The Collected Works / edited by Laurie J. Sampsel.

(Music of the new American nation; 11)

ISBN 0-8153-2408-1

Musical scores are "out of scope" of the Library of Congress's Cataloging-in-Publication program.

ISBN 13: 978-0-8153-2408-9 (hbk)

Table of Contents

Introduction to the Series

This series presents the music of early American composers of sacred music—psalmody, as it was called—in collected critical editions. Each volume has been prepared by a scholar who has studied the musical history of the period and the stylistic qualities of the composer. The purpose of the series is to present the music of important early American composers in accurate editions for both performance and study. Until now, much of this repertory was unavailable except in the original tunebooks in which the music was first issued. These are difficult to use because of their age and fragility, the antique layout of the musical typography, and frequent printing errors that beset the music and text. While the music is presented here in modern musical orthography, no attempt has been made to improve it. Suspected typographical errors have been corrected (and noted in the commentary), but what may be thought of as compositional errors—parallel fifths and octaves, for example—are an important part of the musical style and have not been tampered with.

The twenty-three composers represented in this series were among the most important of the several hundred who contributed to the psalmody repertory. Some, like Abraham Wood, Joseph Stone, Jacob French, and Elisha West, were prolific and popular in their day but are largely unknown today. Others, such as Nathaniel Billings, Lewis Edson, Jr., and Merit Woodruff, were little known even in their own time, but they wrote some interesting and expressive music that warrants wider acquaintance. Most of these composers have the whole of their published music presented in this series. This will allow for a better assessment of their musical contributions, and will provide performers with the widest possible selection of the composers' works.

Three particularly prolific composers, Samuel Holyoke, Jacob Kimball, and Oliver Holden, are only represented by selected works. Some criteria used in selecting their pieces to be included here are: which works were popular and influential in the composer's own day and which works represent music of significant artistic merit. Composers who already have collected works editions either in print or in progress—William Billings, Daniel Read, Timothy Swan, and Stephen Jenks—have not been included in this series.

The fifteen volumes in this series by no means exhaust the repertory. A number of significant composers of the era could not be represented, among them Amos Albee, William Cooper, Samuel Capen, Ebenezer Child, Benjamin Holt, Solomon Howe, Jeremiah Ingalls, Walter Janes, Abraham Maxim, Hezekiah Moors, James Newhall, Warwick Palfray, Amos Pilsbury, Zedekiah Sanger, Oliver Shaw, Nehemiah Shumway, Samuel Thomson, and Truman Wetmore. Most of these composers published tunebooks containing their own music and that of colleagues. However, the twenty-three composers whose works are included were important and influential in their day and composed music that has interest and artistic worth in our own.

During the quarter century following the Revolutionary War, a flowering of American musical creativity occurred that was unprecedented in any period until the present day. Centered in the New England states, principally Massachusetts and Connecticut, this outpouring was based on the musical practices of the Congregational church as they had developed over the previous half century. It involved music for the church choir, which had been introduced following over a century of opposition, and its ancillary organizations, the singing school and the musical society. The composers writing for these groups were their friends and neighbors. They supplied pieces for special occasions, for didactic purposes, or as artistic responses to particularly moving psalms or hymns.

These composers were not trained professionals with highly developed skills, but merchants, schoolteachers, farmers, and mechanics who had gained some facility at singing. They learned their compositional craft through trial and observation. They often taught the rudiments of music reading and choral singing to young people in their community in occasional singing schools. Frequently, they also led the choir in their local church. Occasionally they may have been called upon to supply new music for ordinations, celebrations, and other local occasions, or they may have composed pieces to demonstrate musical precepts in their singing schools. Over time, some of these composers amassed a sizable body of works. Friends and supporters then may have encouraged them to publish a tunebook of their pieces. Others, having gained a reputation as a good composer, may have lacked sufficient financial backing to issue a tunebook of their own. Their tunes might then be published in the tunebooks of other compilers. New American music was in demand by singers, and in this way, between about 1780 and 1810, some 200 American composers issued over 5000 pieces—psalm tunes, extended tunes, fuging-tunes, set-pieces, and anthems. Undoubtedly many works remained in manuscript, and, since these lacked the permanence of print, much of this music was lost or destroyed by later generations that generally lacked an appreciation of its historic or aesthetic value. But 5000 pieces is a sizable repertory, one that offers today's choral director a profusion of beautiful, exciting, significant religious partsongs that are again highly valued.

Prior to the Second World War, little notice was taken of early American psalmody. Following the war, however, greater attention began to be paid by scholars to the history, bibliography, and style of this music. Doctoral dissertations by Allen P. Britton and Alan Buechner explored important aspects of this musical tradition. Dissertations and books by Glenn Wilcox, Lawrence Willhide, David McKay, Richard Crawford, David McCormick, Vinson Bushnell, Marvin Genuchi, David Warren Steel, Betty Bandel, and Daniel Jones dealt with individual composers, their lives, and their music. Works by Ralph Daniel, Karl Kroeger, and Nym Cooke have clarified musical forms and personal relationships. The bibliography of Britton, Lowens, and Crawford has provided an accurate account of tunebook publication to 1810.

What has been lacking up to now have been reliable editions of the music. Prior to 1977, the psalmody repertory had received no critical attention. In that year the first volume of *The Complete Works of William Billings,* edited by Hans Nathan, was published by The American Musicological Society and The Colonial Society of Massachusetts. During the 1980s and early 1990s, three more volumes of Billings's music were issued by these societies. Meanwhile, plans were underway for a series of volumes, *Music of the United States of America,* containing American musical monuments. Sponsored by the American Musicological Society, this series will include collected works editions of psalmodists Daniel Read and Timothy Swan. The *Recent Researches in American Music* series, published by A-R Editions, has also issued a volume of music by Stephen Jenks. *Music of the New American Nation* will complement and extend beyond these earlier publications to composers who did not find a place there. Thus, as the twentieth century closes, the works of the most important American psalmodists will be available for performance and study.

Psalmody served a number of functions in eighteenth- and early nineteenth-century America: it was a pious duty in the praise of God, a vehicle for vocal instruction, a means of innocent recreation, both public and private, and a medium for artistic self-expression. The church-goer in the pew probably thought little about the music being sung, so long as it was appropriately solemn and suited to the occasion; however, for the singer in the choir, the singing master, and the composer, it was an important adjunct to daily life. For composers, in particular, psalmody offered a means of communicating their concerns and their vision to a wider audience. Composers set texts that moved them. This can be amply demonstrated by their selection; often these are not the first stanzas of the psalm or hymn, but an interior verse that carries a particularly dramatic image or pressing thought. Their settings are also individual. One composer might set the text as a plain tune, simple and unadorned; another as an extended tune, with expressive melismas; a third as a fuging-tune, with extensive word painting. The same text might also be used in a set-piece, where the musical details are so individual that another text could not be substituted. If the composers were merely concerned with providing a succession of notes to guide a text through time, a purely utilitarian function, they need not have marked them with their own individual expressive features. If they had wanted only to demonstrate some musical precept to their singing schools, they need not have worked to make their tunes melodically expressive and rhythmically invigorating. The American composers of psalmody were artists, somewhat naive perhaps and certainly not as well trained and deeply experienced as European art-music composers, but they approached their medium and performers with the same sense of concern and respect as those who composed symphonies, quartets, and sonatas.

Acknowledgments

I wish to express my appreciation to my colleagues Richard Crawford, William Kearns, Lawrence Worster, and Daniel Jones for their help and encouragement in connection with this project. In particular, I acknowledge my debt to Gary M. Rader, developer of the MusicEase music notation software used for the musical scores. He offered his technical help in overcoming numerous format problems and his expertise in computer operations made the inputting of the music easier. Mary Louise Van Dyke of the Dictionary of American Hymnology assisted in locating some particularly obscure hymn texts. To all of these, plus the editors of the individual volumes, who participated in this project with enthusiasm, I send my deepest thanks.

K.K.

I'd like to express my thanks to the following institutions and individuals whose assistance was invaluable to this project: The New England Historic Genealogical Society, especially Jerome Anderson; The Dictionary of American Hymnology Project at Oberlin College Library, especially Mary Louise VanDyke; The Harvard Divinity School Library, especially Timothy Driscoll; and the American Antiquarian Society, especially Joanne Chaison and Marie Lamoureux.

L. J. S.

Works Cited

Bandel, Betty. *Sing the Lord's Song in a Strange Land: The Life of Justin Morgan*. East Rutherford, NJ: Fairleigh Dickinson University Press, 1981.

Britton, Allen P. "Theoretical Introductions in American Tunebooks to 1800." Ph.D. dissertation, University of Michigan, 1949.

———, Irving Lowens, and Richard Crawford. *American Sacred Music Imprints, 1698–1810: A Bibliography*. Worcester, MA: American Antiquarian Society, 1990.

Buechner, Alan C. "Yankee Singing Schools and the Golden Age of Choral Music in New England." Ph.D. dissertation, Harvard University, 1960.

Bushnell, Vinson C. "Daniel Read of New Haven

Cooke, Nym. "American Psalmodists in Contact and Collaboration (1770–1820)." Ph.D. dissertation, University of Michigan, 1990.

Crawford, Richard. *Andrew Law: American Psalmodist.* Evanston, IL: Northwestern University Press, 1968.

Daniel, Ralph P. *The Anthem in New England before 1800*. Evanston, IL: Northwestern University Press, 1966.

Genuchi, Marvin C. "The Life and Music of Jacob French." Ph.D. dissertation, University of Iowa, 1964.

Jones, Daniel C. L. "Elias Mann (1750–1825): Massachusetts Composer, Compiler, and Singing Master." Ph.D. dissertation, University of Colorado, 1991.

Kroeger, Karl. "The Worcester Collection of Sacred Harmony and Sacred Music in America, 1786–1803." Ph.D. dissertation, Brown University, 1976.

McCormick, David W. "Oliver Holden, Composer and Anthologist." S.M.D. dissertation, Union Theological Seminary, 1963.

McKay, David P., and Richard Crawford. *William Billings of Boston: Eighteenth-Century Composer.* Princeton, NJ: Princeton University Press, 1975.

Steel, David Warren. "Stephen Jenks (1772–1856): American Composer and Tunebook Compiler." Ph.D. dissertation, University of Michigan, 1982.

Wilcox, Glenn C. "Jacob Kimball, Jr. (1761–1826): His Life and Works." Ph.D. dissertation, University of Southern California, 1957.

Willhide, J. Lawrence. "Samuel Holyoke, American Music-Educator." Ph.D. dissertation, University of Southern California, 1954.

Performance Practice

A full appreciation of the music of early American psalmodists depends, to a large extent, upon an understanding of the performance practices applicable to it. Most psalmodists were experienced composers who wrote for a medium they understood from years of practice: the unaccompanied choir of mixed voices. They followed certain conventions of notation and execution that, if followed by today's choirs, enhance the music's aural appeal and communicative powers. This résumé of performance practice in early American psalmody covers the basic elements of the choral sound, the effect of the words, the musical symbols used, ornamentation, and accompaniment. A fuller discussion of these and other issues related to the performance of this music can be found in *The Complete Works of William Billings* (v.4, xxxiii–lxiv).

THE CHORAL MEDIUM

The New England sacred music composer wrote for a choir of mixed voices, normally in four parts, referred to as treble, counter, tenor, and bass. These generally correspond to the soprano, alto, tenor, and bass parts of today's choral ensembles. The main melody of the piece was usually carried by the tenor, sung by male voices. The bass was also a male singing part. The counter was often sung by young boys, who would be reassigned to tenor or bass after their voices broke. The counter also included some deeper female voices, but the majority of female singers were assigned to the treble. A few composers, like William Billings and Isaac Lane, advocated doubling the tenor part an octave higher by a few treble voices and the treble part an octave lower by a few tenors. It is uncertain how widely this arrangement was practiced, since it is mentioned by no other writers. A few composers, like Amos Bull, substituted a second treble part for the counter. In this case, the part would be sung by women and its range would overlap with that of the first treble.

Some composers, such as Samuel Holyoke, Samuel Babcock, and Timothy Olmsted, composed music in only three parts: treble, tenor, and bass. In this arrangement, the principal melody was usually in the treble voice, although it sometimes appeared in the tenor. The composer of three-part music often marked the principal part with the word "Air" to indicate its primacy. A few pieces exist in the repertory for five, six, or seven parts, but these are very rare. Similarly, pieces were occasionally published in only two parts, melody and bass. In most cases, however, these are reductions of four-part pieces, published in this way to permit a larger number to be printed.

The normal church choir of the day probably consisted of from fifteen to thirty singers—perhaps a few more in larger congregations, a few less in smaller. The choir make-up seems to have included a large proportion of male singers. Most writers of the day recommended that at least half the voices be assigned to the bass part, with the rest spread fairly evenly among the other parts. This produced a male-dominated vocal sound with the main melody in the tenor and a special emphasis on the bass. The female voices were apparently relegated to the background. This situation seems to have changed in the early 1800s, however, with the introduction of the principal melody in the treble. In this case, the female voices would lead and the male voices would support the melody.

THE WORDS

The texts for singing were drawn principally from two sources: the psalms and hymns of Isaac Watts and the *New Version of the Psalms* by Nicholas Brady and Nahum Tate. The latter, the metrical translation officially sanctioned by the Anglican Church, was perhaps more widely used before the Revolutionary War, but following it, Watts's version, along with his hymns, gained almost unrivaled ascendancy. A few other English hymnodists contributed to the pool of texts that American composers set: Philip Doddridge, James Relly, Elizabeth Rowe, Ann Steele, Charles Wesley, John Newton, and William Cowper were among the most prominent. But their contributions were minor compared to the overwhelming popularity of Watts. Very few American poets were part of the text pool (e.g., Mather Byles, Jeremy Belknap, Timothy Dwight, and William Billings), and their contributions were very small.

The text played a controlling role in the performance of the music. Not only did it convey the sense of the subject being sung, but it also affected the tempo, dynamics, and mood of the music. Although writers emphasized the effect of the words on performance, the text that was printed with a tune was not necessarily the one that was sung. Substitution of texts performed in public worship was a common practice of the day. Nor was every verse of a psalm or hymn sung. Some stanzas could be omitted without damaging the sense of the subject. A joyous text was to be sung to a joyous tune, set in a major mode with vigorous rhythmic motion. Similarly, a lamenting text required a minor-mode tune, with a moderate to slow pace. Some psalmodists even recommended changing the tempo of a tune if the mood of the text changed from verse to verse. The words could also affect the dynamics of the music. Those conveying strong images, such as "might," "strength," and "power," were to be sung louder than those conveying milder images, such as "weak," "poor," and "lowly." Ejaculatory words, such as "Oh," "Ah," and "Hark," were also to receive extra emphasis. Much was left to the taste and discretion of the choir leader, but his decisions were guided by the subject of the hymn and the words being sung.

MUSICAL SYMBOLS

Most of the notational symbols used in psalmody are familiar to today's singers, although some carried somewhat different meanings than current usage. One of the most important symbols was the time signature. This not only controlled the metrical content of the measures but also determined the tempo of the music. Each time signature carried with it a tactus, an implied tempo, that singers followed to determine how fast or slow to sing. There were nine time signatures in common usage, categorized in so-called moods of time: common, triple, and compound. Common time had four moods, marked C, ₵, reversed C, and 2/4; triple time, three moods, marked 3/2, 3/4, and 3/8; and compound time, two moods, marked 6/4 and 6/8. Within each category, the moods were successively faster. For example, in the first mood of common time (marked C), the quarter-note was to occupy one second of time. The second mood, also with a quarter-note as its beat note, was about half again as fast. The third mood, which had a half-note beat, was also to take a second of time per beat. And the fourth mood, with a quarter-note as the beat note, was to take a full second of time per measure. Triple and compound time were similarly proportioned. A more accurate approximation of tempo could be obtained from the swing of a pendulum keyed to the moods of time, and many tunebook compilers provided pendulum lengths in their discussions of this subject. A summary of metronome markings, based on verbal directions and pendulum swings, is given in *The Complete Works of Billings* (v.4, xlix, lxx).

The tempo suggested by the time signature could be altered by the text being sung—as noted earlier, a lamenting text might be sung slower than indicated, and a joyous text somewhat faster. The tempo might also be altered by the composer's use of directive words, such as *fast, slow, vivace,* and *grave.* These directive words were intended to affect the basic tempo set by the time signature, speeding up or slowing down the tempo by perhaps as much as a quarter to a third.

Because the choir had no conductor (the choir leader acted as leading singer rather than conductor), and each singer kept his or her own time by raising and lowering the hand, tempo fluctuations, such as those associated with *accelerando* and *ritardando,* were not employed in psalmody. Apparently, even at the conclusion of a piece there was no slowing down, except where the composer actually wrote longer note values.

DYNAMICS

Composers of psalmody used dynamic markings only when they intended a special dynamic effect. Otherwise, the text being sung and the musical situation that prevailed determined the dynamic level. If a dynamic mark was used, a single word—*piano, forte, fortissimo*—was placed above the treble staff. This indication affected all the voices singing at that time. Dynamic change was abrupt; *crescendo* and *diminuendo* were seldom used in this music, except in the fuging-tune. When no dynamic mark was present, the choirs sang at a moderate dynamic level, which might be characterized in today's usage by the term *mezzoforte*. *Piano* would be a degree softer, and *forte* a degree louder, with *fortissimo* being as loud as the choir could sing and still maintain a good choral sound. Other dynamic gradations, such as *pianissimo, mezzopiano,* and *mezzoforte,* were rarely used.

Certain musical situations called for certain dynamic levels. If some of the voice parts were silent for a phrase or two, those still singing were supposed to sing their parts *piano*. When the full chorus entered again, it should enter *forte*. It was recommended that the third line of a four-line hymn be sung soft, with the following fourth line sung loud. As the voices joined in the fuge of a fuging-tune, they were to begin softly and increase in strength as they entered, giving the effect of a crescendo. While few specific directions were given by the composers, the perceptive choir leader could fashion a dynamic, vibrant musical performance based on clues provided by the words, the musical texture, and custom.

ORNAMENTATION

Improvised ornamentation of psalm tunes was an American tradition dating back at least to the late seventeenth century. The uncontrolled improvised embellishment of melodies was a motivation for the Boston clerics beginning singing schools in the 1720s. A congregation of voices, each singing the melody as it pleased the singer, must have raised a din that was exhilarating to the participant but dismaying to the listener. Realizing that singers would ornament tunes as they pleased, composers attempted to exert some measure of control over the number and placement of ornaments.

By the late eighteenth century only two graces were widely recommended in tunebook introductions: the trill and the transition. The trill, the rapid alternation between a principal note and its upper neighbor, was sometimes indicated in the music, usually at cadence points. However, it could also be improvised by the performer, and some compilers supplied rules in their tunebooks for adding improvised trills, usually accompanied by a warning not to trill "promiscuously"—a caution to which singers likely paid little heed.

The one ornament that received universal approbation from the tunebook compilers was the transition. This was usually an improvised ornament, although occasionally transitions are notated as cue-size notes slurred from the prior main note and filling in a vocal leap of a third (rarely a fourth or larger interval). The pitch of the transition note was to be touched on quickly and lightly, as a graceful sliding between the two main pitches. The only time a transition was proscribed was when a "mark of distinction" (a wedge-shaped staccato mark, performed as an accent) stood over the notes. Then the vocal portamento was not to be performed.

Some of the younger psalmodists of the 1790s and early 1800s employed the appoggiatura, particularly at phrase endings. Appoggiaturas were notated as cue-size eighth- or quarter-notes on the beat and slurred to the following main note. Eighth- and quarter-note appoggiaturas seem to have been used interchangeably. Their value was determined by that of the following note: if the following note was a duple value, the appoggiatura took half; if triple, the appoggiatura took two-thirds.

ACCOMPANIMENT

Psalmody was composed originally as unaccompanied choral music. The tunebooks rarely contain separate instrumental parts or bass figures that would suggest a keyboard accompaniment. Most Congregational churches in New England had long opposed the use of instruments in the meetinghouse and came to accept them only as an expedient to support weak singing. During the 1790s some pastors, concerned over the deteriorating vocal part of the service, asked members of the congregation who could play certain instruments to sit in the choir and support the weak parts. The instruments commonly used were the "bass viol" (i.e., cello) or bassoon to double the bass, the flute or clarinet to help the counter, and the flute or violin to assist the treble. The tenor might also have been doubled by clarinet or viola. The instruments usually played with the singers, although they were occasionally permitted to play over the tune before the singers entered. Rarely, the choral sections of a composition were connected by an instrumental "symphony" (a brief passage without underlaid text) that shared one or more staves with the vocal parts.

The question often arises in modern performance whether or not early American psalmody should be performed with instruments. The answer is a matter of individual taste. If the choir is able to present a good performance without instrumental assistance, that is probably preferred. However, choir directors should not avoid the use of instruments for fear of being inauthentic. There is ample evidence that instruments were used in the singing galleries, in particular the bass viol to support the bass voices. If the church possesses an organ, that instrument might be used to accompany both the choir and congregation singing. There is no record of the piano or harpsichord being employed to accompany the singing, although they may have been used in the home when this music was performed there. An organist accompanying psalmody must take care to play from the open score or a transcription of it. In particular, the bass line should not be thought of as an unfigured bass. Since the contrapuntal procedures used by the composers do not conform to thoroughbass rules, the music does not follow those principles and dissonance will result from adhering to them.

Much in the performance of early American psalmody was left to the taste and judgment of the performers. This obviously led to a wide variation in the quality of individual performances. Following directions, however faithfully, cannot, of course, guarantee good performances, yet ignoring them can often distort the music. American psalmodists wrote a music that embodied their faith, hopes, aspirations, and visions, in an effort to communicate these to the singers and listeners. It is most respectful of their efforts for present-day performers to sing their music in a style that enhances these qualities. However, the important thing in all musical performance is to seek to capture and convey the music's spirit. It should be musically convincing to the listener, and, if it is, that spirit will move both performers and listeners.

Editorial Policy

ORGANIZATION OF THE EDITION

Each volume of the series presents the music of either one composer or several composers who worked at about the same time in the same region. Each composer's works are presented in alphabetical order by title. This arrangement overrides the original format in which some of the music was published—in collections with their own importance and integrity. However, many of the pieces are taken from different collections, most of which contained compositions of many other composers. Except in a few cases where the tunebook contained only the music of a single composer, there is little reason to retain the original order of pieces in a volume. Each volume begins with a brief introduction to the series, performance practice, the composer and his music, and this statement of general editorial policy. Following the music, a commentary on the pieces and various indexes are included.

SOURCES

The sources of all works included in this edition are tunebooks and other musical publications issued between ca. 1780 and ca. 1810 by American printers. Manuscripts, of which few survive, do not usually contain definitive versions of the pieces, because the composer often revised them when preparing a collection for printing. Tunes were often reprinted in different tunebooks, occasionally with some variation in their musical detail. In choosing which versions most clearly represent the composers' intentions, the following criteria have been observed:

1. A tunebook for which the composer was also the compiler has been given the highest priority. This seems likely best to represent the composer's intentions. If the composer printed the work several times, the latest printing is considered the definitive version. Variants in the earlier versions are discussed in the commentary.

2. A tunebook with which the composer seems likely to have had some connection, even though he was not the compiler, is given the second highest priority. This is often the earliest printing of a work, and thus is likely to represent the composer's intentions. Later printings, often reprinted from this version, have usually not been considered.

3. The earliest printing of a work has been selected if neither of the previous criteria apply.

MUSICAL ORTHOGRAPHY

Slurs and ties

Slurs indicating a melisma (two or more notes sung to one syllable) have not been used in this edition. Instead, the placement of syllables and a line extending from the last letter of a word indicate the melisma's length. In some cases, several repeated notes appear under a slur in the publication. If these notes are separated by a bar line, the slur is interpreted as a tie, which is supplied editorially. Repeated notes may also occur within a bar; in most such instances, the notes are not treated as tied, but should be articulated in performance. In some instances, however, repeated notes within a bar under a slur have been considered as ties: when the repeated notes constitute a notational value for which a single symbol is unavailable (such as the value of five eighth-notes). Such articulated repeated notes are mentioned in the commentary; ties, however, have been added without comment.

In the few cases where only one note of a "chusing note" (a two- or three-note chord in one vocal part) is tied, ties on the other notes have been tacitly supplied.

Accidentals

Psalmodists were often inconsistent in applying accidentals in their music, particularly leading tones in pieces in minor keys, less frequently on the fourth scale degree in major keys. Billings noted in *The Continental Harmony* that the seventh scale degree in minor was usually raised in performance whether it was indicated or not. While such alterations have not been made editorially to this edition, accidental sharps may be added in performance as personal preference dictates. Editorial accidentals in parentheses are supplied to clarify passages where notational practice of the day required none. Composers sometimes used both the raised and lowered form of a pitch simultaneously, apparently on purpose. In such cases, an accidental natural sign has been supplied by the editor.

During this period, sharps and flats not in the key signature seem to have affected only the notes before which they stood. Thus, one frequently finds several chromatically altered, repeated notes in succession, each with its own sharp or flat. In this edition, modern practice is applied: accidentals affect all notes on that pitch for the duration of the measure, and extra accidentals have been tacitly omitted. Composers occasionally used sharps and flats as substitutes for the natural sign, to cancel temporarily a sharp or flat in the key signature. This usage has been interpreted as calling for a natural sign, which has been supplied without comment.

Clef signs

American psalmodists normally used three clef signs in their music: treble clef for treble and tenor voices, alto clef for counter, and bass clef for the bass. The treble clef in the tenor was intended to be sung an octave lower than the notated pitch. In this edition, clefs for the treble and bass have been retained, the treble clef substituted for the alto clef in the counter, and the octavating treble clef supplied to the tenor. Occasionally, the treble clef was also used in the counter voice, with the music notated an octave higher than it was intended to be sung. In such cases, the counter line has been transposed an octave lower.

Meter signatures

The meter signatures used in this edition are those which the composers employed, with one exception: the third mood of common time, indicated either by a reversed C or a reversed C with a line through it, has not been retained and the time signature 2/2 tacitly substituted. Performers are reminded that, in addition to specifying the metrical organization of the music, meter signatures in psalmody also indicated tempo (see Performance Practice).

Repeat signs

The sign :S: was usually used to indicate the beginning of a section of music to be repeated. Normally placed above the treble line, the sign was intended to affect all voices. The same sign also indicated the end of the repeated section, except when the end of the repeat coincided with the conclusion of the piece, in which case it was usually omitted. In this edition, the dotted double bar has been substituted without comment. Occasionally the first ending of a repeated section has been adjusted to correct the notation. Such alterations have been noted in the commentary.

Repetitions of words or lines of text were also at times indicated with a repeat sign. These signs have been tacitly omitted and the intended text supplied without mention in the commentary.

An unusual type of fugal repetition is found in a few pieces: staggered repeats in the fugal entries. Normally, in the fugal section of a fuging-tune, all voices repeat back to the onset of the fuge (usually beginning in the bass voice). However, in a few pieces, the repeat goes back to the start of that particular voice, omitting prior rests, and retaining a four-part polyphonic texture throughout. In this edition, the staggered repeats have been written out, the repeat signs omitted, and a note made in the commentary.

TEXTS

Text sources and number of stanzas

Composers normally set a single stanza of text, most often the first stanza, but sometimes a later one. In the present edition, contemporaneous sources of the poetry that has been set, not necessarily the versions printed in the tunebooks, are taken as the standard. During the period many editions of the various hymn collections were printed, making it virtually impossible to determine precisely which one a composer actually used. Although there may occasionally be some small variation in the text of the psalm or hymn, an attempt has been made to find a contemporary source that closely matches the text that the composer set.

Metrical psalters and hymnbooks were widespread, so performers who wanted to sing more stanzas would have had easy access to them. In this edition, additional stanzas of text have been supplied following the music of strophic pieces, providing access to the poem from which the composers drew their text. Where possible, text sources or lyricists have been noted at the head of the music, although these may have been omitted in the original publication. Complete information on text sources and number of stanzas set is included in the commentary.

When the composer set a stanza of a text other than the first, that stanza has been designated stanza one and the remaining stanzas renumbered to follow. Composers also occasionally set two or, rarely, three stanzas of text, but still intending strophic performance. In such cases, all of the text that was set is considered to be the first stanza, and later stanzas have been combined and renumbered to parallel the first. All such information is presented in the commentary.

Composers' strophic settings of multiple stanzas sometimes left one stanza unset. Such stanzas, usually the last in the hymn, have been placed in the commentary, where performers may sing them with the music as they wish. For the additional stanzas of text, following contemporaneous sources, left margins have been justified and the first letters of each line capitalized.

Poetical Meter indications

Psalm tunes and fuging-tunes were designed to be sung strophically. In many cases, the tunes could also be used with completely different texts from the one the composer set. At the head of many tunes are letters designating the poetic meter the tune is intended to serve. There were four standard meter designations in Anglo-American psalmody:

L.M. = Long Meter (4 lines of 8 syllables each in iambic meter).

C.M. = Common Meter (4 lines alternating 8 and 6 syllables each in iambic meter).

S.M. = Short Meter (4 lines of 6, 6, 8, and 6 syllables, respectively, in iambic meter).

H.M. = Hallelujah Meter (4 lines of 6 syllables each, followed by 4 lines of 4 syllables each, in iambic meter).

A fifth designation—P.M.—stands for Particular Meter, which could be any syllable pattern that does not conform to one of the four standard meters. In this edition, the four standard designations are used without further explanation, but P.M. is followed by the exact syllable pattern given in brackets.

Spelling, capitalization, and punctuation

The spelling and punctuation of the text follow the poetic source. In some publications, composers tend to use phonetic spellings and word abbreviations to save space on crowded copper plates and to use sporadic punctuation. Significant differences in spelling between the underlaid text and the text source have been noted in the commentary, but obvious misspellings have been tacitly altered. Changes in punctuation have been made without comment.

Capitalization also tends to be sporadic. In most eighteenth-century poetic sources, the first letter of each line of a verse is capitalized, a practice retained in this edition. Occasionally other words, such as nouns, adjectives, and prepositions, begin with a capital letter in the tunebooks for no apparent reason; these have not been retained, except for proper names and direct references to the Deity. Metaphorical references to God or Jesus—e.g., savior, redeemer, creator, and judge—and pronoun references to them, often capitalized in the text source, have been spelled with lowercase letters without mention.

Names that are sometimes printed in italic type in the text source have been printed here in roman type. Quotation marks, usually set at the beginning of every line containing quoted words, are here placed at the beginning and end of the quotation, and at the beginning of each subsequent stanza if the quotation extends beyond a single verse.

Partial texts

Because of space constraints on tunebook pages, engravers sometimes indicated only the first few words of the text, leaving it to the performers to find the remaining words in psalm and hymn books. In particular in fuging sections, the full text was usually set under one voice, normally the counter, and only the beginning words of the text were printed in the other voices. In this edition, the full text fitting the music has been set in all voices without mention in the commentary. Even when limited space was not a consideration, the repetition of the prior line was often indicated by only the first two or three words of that line. Such repetitions have been written out in full.

Contractions and abbreviations

To save space, long words were often contracted in the tunebooks and, occasionally, in the text sources. In most cases, contractions—such as "tho'" for "though" and "thro'" for "through"—have been tacitly spelled out in full. Contractions have been retained when a word of several syllables is set to be sung to fewer syllables—e.g., "heav'n" for "heaven" and "sov'reign" for "sovereign." "Ye" was often used as an abbreviation for the article "the"; in such cases "the" has been tacitly restored. However, when "ye" has been used as an archaic form of "you" it has been retained. One also encounters similar abbreviations for other common words—such as "yt" for "that" and "wch" for "which"—which have been restored to their modern spelling without comment.

OTHER ISSUES

Initial measure of rest

In some works a measure of rest is placed at the beginning of a tune. The composer apparently intended a measure's silence to be observed between the end of the underlaid text and the beginning of the next stanza to be sung. (Singers would normally continue beating time between stanzas, assuring a precise beginning to the next stanza.) These rests were almost always omitted in later reprints of the piece, and they have been tacitly omitted in this edition.

Notation of dotted notes

In 6/4 and 6/8 time the values of the dotted whole-note and dotted half-note, respectively, were often notated as two dotted half-notes or two dotted quarter-notes tied. In 3/2 and 3/4 time, however, the dotted whole-note and dotted half-note were used. In this edition, in 6/4 and 6/8 time, dotted whole-notes and dotted half-notes are substituted without comment.

Beaming of note groups

The beaming of groups of notes tends to be erratic in tunebooks. Normally an eighth-note (or smaller value) carrying a single syllable of text is not connected to the next note following it, but in melismas, where the single syllable may extend for two, three, four, or more eighth-notes (or other smaller values), the beaming may encompass all of the notes, some of them, or notes may be flagged separately under a slur. In this edition, beaming follows the meter of the music, so that in 2/2 time four eighth-notes sung on one syllable would be beamed as a group. No mention is made of beaming discrepancies in the commentary.

Rebarring

Occasionally, it has been necessary to rebar either whole pieces or parts of them, so that the musical and textual accents coincide. Particularly in anthems, where the prose text presented the composers with an irregular succession of verbal accents, some psalmodists were unable to coordinate their music to the stresses in the text. However, psalmodists generally subscribed to the axiom that whenever the words and music did not coincide, the accents of the words prevailed. Thus, the editor has adjusted the meters and barlines to align the accents of the words and those of the music. Whenever a piece or a passage has been rebarred, a note of the alteration has been made in the commentary for that work, and the original meter signature and barring have been indicated above the treble line for the length of the rebarring.

Introduction to This Volume

This volume contains the collected works of Samuel Babcock (ca. 1760–1813), an active and talented Boston-area composer. Babcock is known primarily for his tunebook, *Middlesex Harmony*, which included only his own compositions and was published in two editions (1795 and 1803). *Middlesex Harmony* was one of six single-composer collections of sacred music published by Thomas and Andrews during the period 1791–1795 (Crawford, *Hardening* 19). Babcock contributed a relatively high number of pieces to the repertory of American psalmody. This edition includes seventy-five works known to be by Babcock, as well as six of doubtful attribution. Perhaps what is most interesting, however, is his response to the growing clamor for the reform and "improvement" of traditional New England psalmody during his time. Rather than choosing either to maintain the traditional methods or adopt the newer Methodist style of psalmody, as many of his contemporaries did, Babcock combined elements of both to create an individual approach.

The Life and Music of Samuel Babcock

Many details of Samuel Babcock's life are still unknown. He was probably one of two first cousins: either the Samuel born to John and Rachel Badcock in Milton, Massachusetts, in 1760, or the Samuel born to George and Ruth Badcock in Sudbury, Massachusetts, in 1761. His generation seems to have been the first to change the spelling of the name to Babcock (Appleton 7). Our Samuel Babcock married Elizabeth Swift on 20 October 1783, in Cambridge, Massachusetts, and his first son, also Samuel, was born there on 22 May 1785 (Baldwin 1:31 and v.2). A few years later the family moved to Watertown, about six miles up the Charles River from Boston, where Babcock spent most of his adult life. Three more children were born between 1789 and 1794, two daughters (Sally and Rebecca) and another son (James) (*Watertown Records* 3:170). Sometime between 1810 and 1813, Babcock migrated to the town of French Mills, Bradford County, in north-eastern Pennsylvania. The reasons for this move are unknown, but Babcock, still in his early 50s, died in French Mills on 23 November 1813 (*Columbian Centinel* 15 Dec. 1813).

During his years in Watertown, Babcock was an active craftsman and conscientious citizen, as well as a musician. His main occupation was as a hatter; he bought a shop for that purpose on 21 September 1791 (Cambridge). The *Watertown Records* show his involvement in his community as a constable in 1794 and as a grand juror in 1794 and 1795 (*Watertown Records* 7:71,79,94). His musical activities went beyond composing and tunebook compilation. He served as choir leader at the local Congregational Church and taught singing schools in Watertown in 1798 and 1804 (*Watertown Records* 7:191,345). He may also have been active as an itinerant singing master (Sampsel 112). Babcock sometimes composed music for special occasions. In her history of Watertown, Maud deLeigh Hodges describes the performance of a piece written by Babcock for the town's memorial service for George Washington (77). Although the music is lost, the text written by Rev. Richard Elliot survives (Holden, *Sacred* [5]: *Columbian Centinel* 8 Jan. 1800). Babcock also composed a Masonic song to a text by Thaddeus Mason Harris for the Anniversary of St. John the Baptist, 24 June 5802 (i.e., 1802), which was published in the second edition of *Middlesex Harmony* (hereafter MH2). In the preface of MH2 Babcock noted that the work was written "at the request of a number of gentlemen of that fraternity . . . by their desire, and for their use" (MH2, [ii]). Although not a Mason himself, Babcock seemed proud to participate in this Masonic celebration (Alcorn letter).

The 1795 edition of *Middlesex Harmony* (hereafter MH1) contains twenty-six of his pieces, all first printings. In the preface to MH2 (1803), Babcock noted that the first edition was not intended for use in singing schools, "being published without the rules, and consisting chiefly of music not calculated for that purpose." Babcock probably intended the music to be used in singing societies. By denying that MH1 was intended for singing schools, Babcock seems to imply that MH2 was, indeed, designed for this purpose. The inclusion of the rudiments of a music section also supports this use. MH2 reprints all but one of the works from MH1, along with forty-one new Babcock compositions.

In addition to the *Middlesex Harmony*, first printings of thirteen pieces appear in tunebooks compiled by others. These tunebooks are: Andrew Law's *Select Harmony* (1779), Oliver Holden's *Union Harmony* (1793), Joseph Stone and Abraham Wood's *Columbian Harmony* (1793), Daniel Belknap's *Evangelical Harmony* (1800), Holden's *Plain Psalmody* (1800), and Abijah Forbush's *Psalmodist's Assistant* (2d ed., 1806). Seven of these pieces are thought to be by Samuel Babcock. The other six, SPRINGFIELD, ADMIRATION, SOLITUDE, WARREN, WESTBOROUGH, and WRENTHAM, are of uncertain attribution. Some or all of them may be by Lemuel Babcock, a shadowy central Massachusetts composer and singing master, who was active between ca.1778 and ca.1810. SPRINGFIELD was first printed in Law's *Select Harmony* (1779) with the attribution "Babcock" (see Crawford, *Andrew Law* 310). A variant version of SPRINGFIELD was published along with the other five works noted above in Stone and Wood's *Columbian Harmony* (1793), where all six works were attributed simply to "Babcock." Stone and Wood's collection features compositions by Worcester-area composers, and Lemuel lived in nearby Framingham while Samuel lived near Boston. Further, SOLITUDE was attributed to "L. Babcock" in the third edition of Solomon Howe's *The Young Man's Instructive Companion* (1804–10) as well as in the Waterhouse manuscript compiled in Brookline, Massachusetts, about 1782 (see Crawford and McKay 54). These six pieces exhibit stylistic divergences from those pieces known to be by Samuel Babcock. Because of their uncertain attributions, they have been placed in an appendix in this edition and excluded from the following discussion of Samuel Babcock's musical style.

Babcock showed a strong preference for composing in the extended psalm tune form. Of the seventy-five pieces known to be by him, nearly half (thirty-three) follow this pattern. The plain psalm tune is represented by seventeen pieces. Babcock also composed thirteen set pieces, eight fuging tunes, and four anthems.

Like many younger psalmodists, Babcock showed a predilection for three part vocal textures. Four vocal parts were standard at this time, and some tunebook compilers actually added a fourth part to works for three voices. For example, the preface to the *Worcester Collection* (1791) states that "In order to accommodate the singers of each part of sacred musick, in several instances where a fourth part has been wanting, the Editor has had the deficiency supplied by skillful persons" (*Worcester Collection*). Three-part writing was, however, one of the hallmarks of the Methodist style of psalmody. Babcock composed more than seventy-five percent of his music for three parts.

While a full discussion of the Methodist style is beyond the scope of this introduction, a brief description is in order (see Temperley, Chap.7). In addition to the three-part texture, the Methodist style often places the primary melody in the treble rather than the tenor. The top two voices frequently move in thirds and sixths with melodies that are florid and ornamented. The bass often outlines chord tones or provides a pedal point; it often appears "instrumental" in nature with large leaps and repeated notes. Influenced by theater and dance music, the style is like secular music of the day, with lively rhythms and tempi and catchy melodies. Standard harmonic progressions predominate, and there is less independent counterpoint than in traditional psalmody. Clarity of the text is paramount. The text meters are often unusual, frequently employing lines of seven syllables, seldom found in Congregational and Anglican hymnody. Text and / or music are often repeated. Weak phrase endings are common, as is the formulaic cadence pattern I6/4-V-I.

In addition to composing in three parts and repeating both text and music (typically ABB in the extended form), Babcock's music displays many of the traits of the Methodist style outlined above. For example, his bass lines often seem more instrumental than vocal, suggesting that they were composed simultaneously with the upper parts (for example, see STOW). His counterpoint often consists of parallel thirds or sixths between the tenor and treble voices (see HARVARD). Babcock's melodic lines are typically conjunct, often scalar (again see STOW) or triadic (see EPHRATAH and NORTH-KINGSTON). He tends towards duple meters, particularly 2/4, and fast tempi as well as short note values (typically eighths and sixteenths). However, his music also includes some parallel perfect fifths and octaves, incomplete triads at cadences, and contrapuntally produced dissonances, all traits of the traditional style. A representative and noteworthy tune is the set piece MILTON. Here Babcock uses contrasting textures, dynamics, and tempi to set effectively an expressive text by Watts. The catchy triadic melodies and the alternating use of the bass voice as a harmonic and melodic line are significant characteristics.

Babcock's earlier music seems more experimental than his later works. Some pieces in MH2 appear almost formulaic in their compositional approach. For example, in MH2 Babcock composed all of his extended psalm tunes in ABB form and in duple meter. A similar trend is noticeable in his fuging tunes. In the six three-voice fuging tunes printed after 1800 (ELEVATION, GRATITUDE, LUBEC, PALMER, RESOLUTION, and SUNDAY) the order of imitative entries is invariable (bass, tenor, treble) and all but one uses the same method to bring the parts back together.

Babcock's approach to fuging tunes was innovative in light of the rhetoric of reformers against fuging music. Despite a growing condemnation of the form, Babcock published six of his seven fuging tunes after 1800. In his preface to MH2, Babcock wrote, "He [Babcock] has not consulted his own inclination entirely in introducing fuging music into pieces intended for public worship: But as it has been the general practice, where-ever he has given in to it, he has endeavoured to preserve the sense of the lines entire, so as not to 'make a jargon of words'" (preface). The statement about fuging tunes making "a jargon of words" must be a response to Samuel Holyoke's complaint in the preface to his *Harmonia Americana* (1791) of twelve years earlier. In her study of American fuging tunes, Fawcett-Yeske wrote, "His [Babcock's] later fuging tunes suggest a concern for the clarity of the text and a preference for transparency in texture achieved by writing three- rather than four-voice tunes—concerns and style traits that he decidedly shared with Holden and Holyoke" (333).

Many of Babcock's later works in other forms also exhibit a great sensitivity to the texts being set and show Babcock's growth as a composer. In his article on text painting in the music of Billings, Kroeger describes five word-painting devices employed by psalmodists: melodic direction, onomatopoeia, pace and tempo, texture, and dynamics (Kroeger). Babcock used each of these devices in his tunes and set pieces, but especially in his later pieces for three parts. For a discussion of subtle, but expressive use of these techniques in CAMBRIDGE, CHRISTMAS, CONSECRATION, ELEVATION, ELIM, MENOTOMY, NORFOLK, QUINCY, RESIGNATION, and SMYRNA, see Sampsel (120–124).

Babcock published four anthems, through-composed settings of biblical prose, the most complex musical form that he attempted. Three of the anthems were first printed in MH1 and were reprinted in MH2 along with a fourth work that appeared there for the first time. In each anthem, 2/4 is the predominant musical meter, and movement in quarter- and eighth-notes is the principal rhythmic motion. The settings are largely syllabic, with few melismas more than two notes in length. Textural contrasts are achieved mostly through homophonic means: solos answered by full chorus, duets in two voices answered by duets in two other voices. There is relatively little independent counterpoint. All of this reflects a conscious concern for the intelligibility of the text.

Two unusual pieces, both from MH1, deserve comment. NEEDHAM and CALEDONIA are among Babcock's best efforts. NEEDHAM is a three-part extended-tune setting of a hymn by John Gambold. Babcock alternated between homophonic texture for the first and third lines and an imitative contrapuntal setting for the second and fourth lines, the fourth line is then repeated homophonically to end the tune. CALEDONIA is the most unusual piece in Babcock's catalog. He used an ostinato bass for the line "I will praise thee" and a catchy, often repeated melodic phrase in the tenor and treble to create an energetic expression of praise.

Samuel Babcock's skill as a composer was substantial. He contributed a sizeable number of pieces to early New England psalmody, although they were published too late to gain admittance to its standard repertory. The publication of only his own music in both editions of *Middlesex Harmony* is a strong indication of his confidence, independence, and creativity. Finally, his approach to the issue of reform is one of synthesis of elements from both the traditional and Methodist styles of psalmody. For these reasons, as well as its intrinsic excellence, Babcock's music is worthy of performance and study today.

Works Cited

Alcorn, Cynthia W. Letter to the author. 8 June 1998.

Appleton, William S. *The Family of Badcock of Massachusetts*. Boston: D. Clapp, 1881.

Babcock, Samuel. *The Middlesex Harmony: Being an Original Composition of Sacred Music, in Three and Four Parts*. Boston: Thomas & Andrews, 1795; 2nd ed. 1803.

Baldwin, Thomas, comp. *Vital Records of Cambridge, Massachusetts to the Year 1850*. Boston: Wright & Potter Print Co., 1914–15.

Belknap, Daniel. *Evangelical Harmony*. Boston: Thomas & Andrews, 1800.

Cambridge County. *Grantees Land Records, 1639–1799*. Book 105. 461–62.

Columbian Centinel and Massachusetts Federalist. 8 Jan. 1800.

Columbian Centinel. 15 Dec. 1813: 2.

Crawford, Richard. "A Hardening of the Categories: 'Vernacular,' 'Cultivated,' and Reactionary in American Psalmody." *American Studies and American Musicology*. New York: Institute for Studies in American Music, 1975.

———. *Andrew Law, American Psalmodist*. Evanston: Northwestern University Press, 1968.

Crawford, Richard, and David P. McKay. "Music in Manuscript: A Massachusetts Tune-book of 1782." *Proceedings of the American Antiquarian Society* 84 (1974): 43–64.

Fawcett-Yeske, Maxine Ann. "The Fuging Tune in America, 1770–1820: An Analytical Study." Ph.D diss., University of Colorado, Boulder, 1997.

Forbush, Abijah. *The Psalmodist's Assistant*. 2nd ed. Boston: Manning & Loring, 1806.

Hodges, Maud deLeigh. *Crossroads on the Charles: A History of Watertown, Massachusetts*. Canaan, N. H.: Published for the Watertown Free Public Library by Phoenix Pub., 1980.

Holden, Oliver. *Plain Psalmody*. Boston: Thomas & Andrews, 1800.

———. *Sacred Dirges, Hymns, and Anthems, Commemorative of the Death of General George Washington*. Boston: Thomas & Andrews, 1800.

———. *Union Harmony, or, Universal Collection of Sacred Music*. Boston: Thomas & Andrews, 1793.

Holyoke, Samuel. *Harmonia Americana*. Boston: Thomas & Andrews, 1791.

Kroeger, Karl. "Word Painting in the Music of William Billings." *American Music* 6 (1988): 41–64.

Law, Andrew. *Select Harmony*. [Cheshire: W. Law?, 1779].

Sampsel, Laurie. "Samuel Babcock: A New England Psalmodist Suspended Between Tradition and Reform." *American Music Research Center Journal* 6 (1996):109–146.

Stone, Joseph, and Abraham Wood. *Columbian Harmony*. [Worcester, 1793].

Temperley, Nicholas. *The Music of the English Parish Church*. 2 vols. Cambridge: Cambridge University Press, 1979.

Watertown Records. Second Book of Births, Marriages and Deaths from 1738 to 1822. Watertown: n.p., 1894.

The Worcester Collection of Sacred Harmony. 3rd ed. Boston: Thomas & Andrews, 1791.

Samuel Babcock : The Collected Works

ANDOVER

John Relly **P. M. [7.6.7.6.7.8.7.6]**

2. I have foolishly abus'd
My saviour's bleeding love;
All thy gifts, my God, misus'd,
When by temptation drove:
Justly I deserve to be
Forsaken by my Lord and God;
Yet shall justice plead for me,
For whom thou shed'st thy blood.

3. Thy blest smiles, my gracious Lord,
Shall cheer my drooping heart;
I'm instructed in thy word
That thou unchanging art:
Draw me to the depth profound
Of all thy sorrows, blood and sweat,
Passing on, through ev'ry wound,
Unto thy mercy seat.

4. There, reclining on thy breast,
Th'eternal sabbath find;
Proving in thee perfect rest
To my poor lab'ring mind!
Waiting till the Lord I see,
And be like him forever pure,
At the heav'nly jubilee
This bliss to me is sure.

ANDOVER

ANTHEM

Comfort Ye, My People

Bible, Isaiah 40

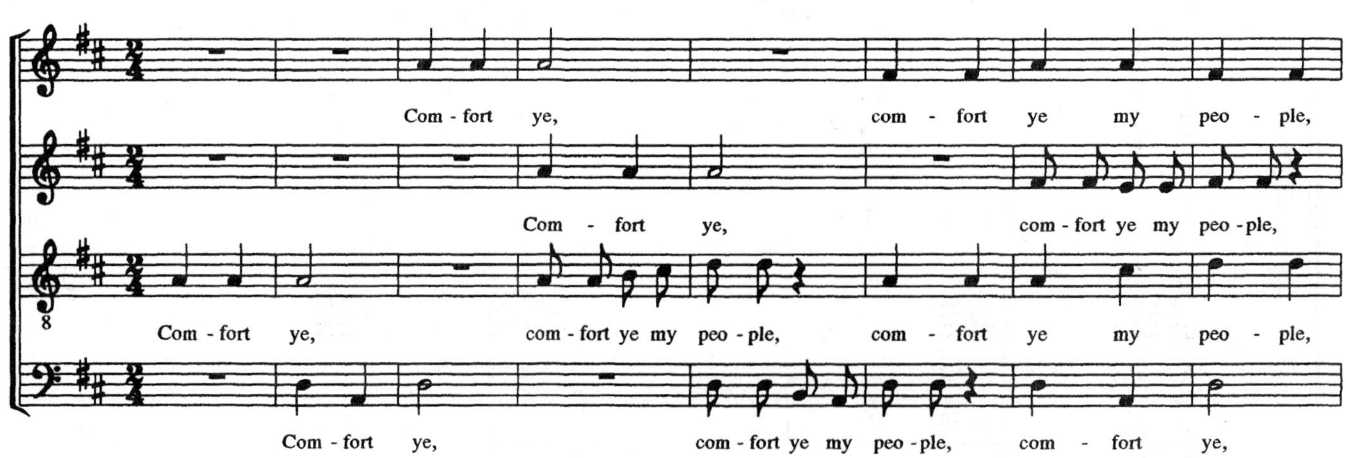

9
com - fort ye my peo - ple, saith your God. Speak
saith your God.
com - fort ye my peo - ple, saith your God. Speak com - fort - a - bly un - to Je -
com - fort ye my peo - ple, saith your God. Speak com - fort - a - bly
17
com - fort - a - bly un - to Je - ru - sa - lem, and
Speak com - fort - a - bly un - to Je - ru - sa - lem,
ru - sa - lem, Speak com - fort - a - bly un - to Je - ru - sa - lem, and cry un - to
un - to Je - ru - sa-lem, Speak com - fort-a-bly un - to Je - ru - sa-lem,
24
cry un - to her that her war - fare is ac - com - plish'd, her sins are par - don'd, her sins are
and cry un - to her that her war - fare is ac - com - plish'd,
her that her war - fare is ac - com - plish'd, that her sins are par - don'd, and cry un-to
Speak com - fort - a - bly un - to Je - ru - sa - lem, and cry un-to

31
par - don'd, her sins are par - don'd, her war - fare is ac - com - plish'd, that her sins are par - don'd, her
her, and cry un - to her that her war - fare is ac - com - plish'd, that her sins are par - don'd, her
her, and cry un - to her that her war - fare is ac - com - plish'd, that her sins are par - don'd, her
38
1.
2.
sins are par - don'd, her sins are par - don'd, par - don'd. For she hath re - ceiv - ed of the Lord's hand
her sins are par - don'd, par - don'd.
sins are par - don'd, her sins are par - don'd, par - don'd.
sins are par - don'd, her sins are par - don'd, par - don'd.
45
dou - ble for all her sins, for she hath re - ceiv - ed of the Lord's hand dou - ble for all her
For she hath re - ceiv - ed of the Lord's hand
For she hath re - ceiv - ed of the Lord's hand dou - ble for all her
For she hath re - ceiv - ed of the Lord's hand dou - ble

53
sins, for she hath re - ceiv - ed of the Lord's hand dou - ble for all her sins.
for she hath re - ceiv - ed of the Lord's hand dou - ble for all her sins.
sins, for she hath re - ceiv - ed of the Lord's hand dou - ble for all her sins.
for she hath re - ceiv - ed of the Lord's hand dou - ble for all her sins.
61
The voice of him that cri - eth in the wild - er - ness: Pre - pare ye the way of the Lord,
69
make straight in the des - ert a high - way for our God, make straight
make straight
make straight

78
Piano
in the des - ert a high - way for our God. Ev' - ry val - ley shall
a high - way for our God.
in the des - ert a high - way for our God.
in the des - ert a high - way for our God. Ev' - ry val - ley shall
86
Cresc.
Forte
be ex - al - ted, and ev' - ry moun - tain and hill made low, Ev' - ry val - ley shall
Ev' - ry val - ley shall
Ev' - ry val - ley shall
be ex - alt - ed, and ev' - ry moun - tain and hill made low, Ev' - ry val - ley shall
94
be ex - alt - ed, and ev' - ry moun - tain and hill made low. And the glo - ry
be ex - alt - ed, and ev' - ry moun - tain and hill made low. And the glo - ry
be ex - alt - ed, and ev' - ry moun - tain and hill made low. And the glo - ry
be ex - alt - ed, and ev' - ry moun - tain and hill made low. And the glo - ry

103
Slow
of the Lord, and the glo - ry of the Lord shall be re - veal - ed, and the
of the Lord, and the glo - ry of the Lord
117
Brisk
glo - ry of the Lord shall be re - veal - ed, and all flesh shall see it, shall
117
1.
2.
see it to - geth - er, and all flesh shall see it to - geth - er, geth - er.
and all flesh shall see it to - geth - er, geth - er.

122
Hal - le - lu - jah, a - men, Hal - le - lu - jah,
Hal - le - lu - jah,
Hal - le - lu - jah, a - men, a - men,
Hal - le - lu - jah, a - men, a - men,

129
a - men, Hal - le - lu - jah, a - men.
a - men, Hal - le - lu - jah, a - men.
Hal - le - lu - jah, Hal - le - lu - jah, a - men.
Hal - le - lu - jah, a - men.

ANTHEM

Lord, Thou Hast Been Our Dwelling Place

Bible, Psalm 90

37
God. and say'st, "Re - turn, ye chil - dren of men," and
God. and say'st, "Re - turn, ye chil - dren of men," and
God. Thou turn-est man to de - struc - tion; and say'st, "Re - turn, ye chil - dren of men," and
47
say'st, "Re - turn, ye chil - dren of men." For all our days are pass - ed a - way in thy wrath: we
say'st, "Re - turn, ye chil - dren of men."
say'st, "Re - turn, ye chil - dren of men."
57
spend our years as a tale that is told. We spend our years as a tale that is told, told.
We spend our years as a tale that is told, told.
We spend our years as a tale that is told, told.
1.
2.
65
So teach us to num - ber our days, to num - ber our
So teach us to num - ber our days, to num - ber our days, to num - ber our
So teach us to num - ber our days, to num - ber our days,

72
days, that we may ap - ply our hearts un - to wis - dom, that we may ap - ply, that we may ap -
days, that we may ap - ply our hearts un - to wis - dom, that we may ap - ply, that we may ap -
that we may ap - ply our hearts un - to wis - dom, that we may ap - ply, that we may ap -

80
1.
2.
ply our hearts un - to wis - dom, that we may ap - ply, ap - ply our hearts un - to wis - dom, wis - dom.
ply our hearts un - to wis - dom, that we may ap - ply our hearts un - to wis - dom, wis - dom.
ply our hearts un - to wis - dom, that we may ap - ply our hearts un - to wis - dom, wis - dom.

ANTHEM

O Come Let Us Sing Unto The Lord

Bible, Psalms 95, 99, and 100

26
1.
2.
en - ter his courts with praise. praise. O come, let us wor-ship and bow down: let us
en - ter his courts with praise. praise. O come, let us wor-ship and bow down: let us
en - ter his courts with praise. praise. O come, let us wor-ship and bow down: let us
en - ter his courts with praise. praise. O come, let us wor-ship and bow down: let us
34
kneel be - fore the Lord our ma - ker, let us kneel be - fore the Lord our ma - ker, For
kneel be - fore the Lord our ma - ker, let us kneel be - fore the Lord our ma - ker,
kneel be - fore the Lord our ma - er, let us kneel be - fore the Lord our ma - ker,
kneel be - fore the Lord our ma - ker, let us kneel be - fore the Lord our ma - ker,
43
he is our God; and we are the peo - ple of his pas - ture, For he is our God; and we are the
For he is our God; and we are the
For he is our God; and we are the
For he is our God; and we are the

51
1.
2.
peo - ple of his pas - ture, pas - ture. Let us come be - fore his pres - ence with thanks - giv - ing, and
peo - ple of his pas - ture, pas - ture. Let us come be - fore his pres - ence with thanks - giv - ing, and
peo - ple of his pas - ture, pas - ture. Let us come be - fore his pres - ence with thanks - giv - ing, and
peo - ple of his pas - ture, pas - ture. Let us come be - fore his pres - ence with thanks - giv - ing, and
57
Slow
en - ter his courts with praise, and en - ter his courts with praise. Ex -
en - ter his courts with praise, and en - ter his courts with praise. Ex -
en - ter his courts with praise, and en - ter his courts with praise. Ex -
en - ter his courts with praise, and en - ter his courts with praise. Ex -
64
alt the Lord our God, and wor - ship at his ho - ly hill; For the Lord our God is
alt the Lord our God, and wor - ship at his ho - ly hill; For the Lord our God is
alt the Lord our God, and wor - ship at his ho - ly hill; For the Lord our God is
alt the Lord our God, and wor - ship at his ho - ly hill; For the Lord our God is

73
1.
2.
ho - ly, For the Lord our God is ho - ly, ho - ly.
ho - ly, For the Lord our God is ho - ly, ho - ly.
ho - ly, For the Lord our God is ho - ly, ho - ly. Ha - le-
ho - ly, For the Lord our God is ho - ly, ho - ly.
82
Hal - le - lu - jah, a - men, Hal - le - lu - jah, a - men, Hal - le - lu - jah, hal - le - lu - jah, a - men,
Hal - le - lu - jah, a - men,
lu - jah, hal - le - lu - jah, hal - le - lu - jah, hal - le-
Hal - le - lu - jah, a - men, Hal - le - lu - jah, hal - le - lu - jah,
90
a - men, Hal - le - lu - jah, hal - le - lu - jah, a - men, a - men.
a - men, Hal - le - lu - jah, a - men, a - men.
lu - jah, hal - le - lu - jah, a - men, a - men.
a - men, Hal - le - lu - jah, a - men, a - men.

ANTHEM

Remember Now Thy Creator

Bible, Ecclesiastes 12

Moderato

26
keep - ers of the house shall trem - ble, and the sound of the grind - ing shall cease: when men shall
keep - ers of the house shall trem - ble, and the sound of the grind - ing shall cease:
keep - ers of the house shall trem - ble, and the sound of the grind - ing shall cease:
keep - ers of the house shall trem - ble, and the sound of the grind - ing shall cease:
35
rise at the voice of the bird, and all the daugh - ters of mu - sic shall be brought low, and all the
and all the
and all the
and all the
44
daugh - ters of mu - sic shall be brought low; be - cause man go - eth to his long
daugh - ters of mu - sic shall be brought low; be - cause man go - eth to his long
daugh - ters of mu - sic shall be brought low; be - cause man go - eth to his long
daugh - ters of mu - sic shall be brought low; be - cause man go - eth to his long

51
home, and mourn - ers go a - bout the streets. Then shall the dust re - turn to the
61
earth as it was, and the spir - it shall re - turn un - to God who gave it, and the
69
spir - it shall re - turn un - to God who gave it. Let us hear the con - clu - sion: Fear

77
God, and keep his com - mand - ments, for this is the du - ty of
God, and keep his com - mand - ments, for this is the du - ty of
God, and keep his com - mand - ments, for this is the du - ty of
God, and keep his com - mand - ments, for this is the du - ty of
83
man, for this is the du - ty of man, Fear God, and
man, for this is the du - ty of man, Fear God, and
man, for this is the du - ty of man, Fear God, and
man, for this is the du - ty of man, Fear God, and
89
keep his com - mand - ments, for this is the du - ty of man.
keep his com - mand - ments, for this is the du - ty of man.
keep his com - mand - ments, for this is the du - ty of man.
keep his com - mand - ments, for this is the du - ty of man.

ASHFORD

John Newton **P. M. [7.7.7.7]**

40
gain the joy - ful sound, Let the na - tions roll it 'round! Zi - on shout, Zi - on
gain the joy - ful sound, Let the na - tions roll it 'round! Zi - on shout, Zi - on
gain the joy - ful sound, Let the na - tions roll it 'round! Zi - on shout, Zi - on
50
shout, Zi - on shout, for this is he, God the sav - iour dwells in thee, For this is
shout, Zi - on shout, for this is he, God the sav - iour dwells in thee, For this is
shout, Zi - on shout, for this is he, God the sav - iour dwells in thee, For this is
60
he, God the sav - iour dwells in thee, God the sav - iour dwells in thee.
he, God the sav - iour dwells in thee, God the sav - iour dwells in thee.
he, God the sav - iour dwells in thee, God the sav - iour dwells in thee.

AUSPICIOUS MORN

Anna Barbauld **C. M.**

BABEL

P. M. [7.7.7.7.7.]

2. On the willows there we hung
Our neglected harps on high,
Silent, useless, and unstrung,
Strangers now to harmony,
Once our pleasure and our joy.

3. Then our proud, triumphant foes,
Haughty, insolent, and gay,
Call'd for music in our woes,
"Sing us some sweet Hebrew lay,
Sacred to some holy day."

4. Cruel foes t'insult us so,
Sunk so deep in helpless grief,
Sighs and tears to vent our woe,
Now our only poor relief,
To the charms of music deaf.

5. O Jerusalem! thy fate,
Wounds my bleeding heart so deep,
Let my trembling hands forget
How the tuneful lyre to sweep,
When for thee I cease to weep.

6. Yet I will not thus repine;
Ev'ry foe to thee shall bend;
Triumph glorious, shall be thine,
All thy woes shall have an end,
God himself will be thy friend.

BABEL

CALEDONIA

John Newton **P. M. [7.7.7.7]**

20
turn'd a - way, ev' - ry day, I will praise thee ev' - ry day.
turn'd a - way, ev' - ry day, I will praise thee ev' - ry day.
turn'd a - way, I will praise thee ev' - ry day.
30
Com - for - ta - ble thoughts a - rise, From the bleed - ing sac - ri - fice, Ev' - ry day
Com - for - ta - ble thoughts a - rise, From the bleed - ing sac - ri - fice, Ev' - ry day
Com - for - ta - ble thoughts a - rise, From the bleed - ing sac - ri - fice, Ev' - ry day
40
I will praise thee ev' - ry day, I will praise thee ev' - ry day, Now thine
I will praise thee ev' - ry day, I will praise thee ev' - ry day, Now thine
I will praise thee, I will praise thee, I will
49
an - ger's turn'd a - way, ev' - ry day, I will praise thee ev' - ry day.
an - ger's turn'd a - way, ev' - ry day, I will praise thee ev' - ry day.
praise thee ev' - ry day, I will praise thee ev' - ry day.

CAMBRIDGE

New Version Psalm 100 **L. M.**

36
en - ter then his tem - ple gates, Thence to his courts de - vout - ly press, And still your grate - ful
en - ter then his tem - ple gates, Thence to his courts de - vout - ly press, And still your grate - ful
en - ter then his tem - ple gates, Thence to his courts de - vout - ly press, And still your grate - ful
46
1.
2.
hymns re - peat, And still his name with prais - es bless, bless. For he's the Lord su - preme - ly
hymns re - peat, And still his name with prais - es bless, bless. For he's the Lord su - preme - ly
hymns re - peat, And still his name with prais - es bless, bless. For he's the Lord su - preme - ly
56
good, His mer - cy is for - ev - er sure; His truth, which all times firm - ly stood, To
good, His mer - cy is for - ev - er sure; His truth, which all times firm - ly stood, To
good, His mer - cy is for - ev - er sure; His truth, which all times firm - ly stood, To
65
Slow
1.
2.
end - less ag - es shall en - dure, To end - less ag - es shall en - dure, dure.
end - less ag - es shall en - dure, To end - less ag - es shall en - dure, dure.
end - less ag - es shall en - dure, To end - less ag - es shall en - dure, dure.

CANA

Anna Barbauld **P. M. [7.7.7.7]**

2. For the blessings of the field,
For the stores the gardens yield,
For the vine's exalted juice,
For the gen'rous olive's use;

3. Flocks that whiten all the plain,
Yellow sheaves of ripen'd grain,
Clouds that drop their fatt'ning dews,
Suns that temp'rate warmth diffuse;

4. All that spring with bounteous hand
Scatters o'er the smiling land:
All that lib'ral autumn pours
From her rich o'erflowing stores;

5. These to thee, our God, we owe,
Source, whence all our blessings flow;
And for these our souls shall raise
Grateful vows and solemn praise.

6. Yet should rising whirlwinds tear
From its stem, the op'ning ear;
Should the fig-tree's blasted shoot
Drop its green untimely fruit;

7. Should the vine put forth no more,
Nor the olive yield her store;
Though the sick'ning flocks should fall,
And the herds desert the stall;

8. Yet to thee our souls shall raise
Grateful vows and solemn praise;
And, when ev'ry blessing's flown,
Love thee for thyself alone.

CANA

CHARITY

Watts Hymns I No.134 **L. M.**

18
Still, I am noth - ing, Still, I am noth - ing with - out love.
Still, I am noth - ing, Still, I am noth - ing with - out love.
Still, I am noth - ing, Still, I am noth - ing with - out love.
Still, I am noth - ing, Still, I am noth - ing with - out love.
23
Should I dis - trib - ute all my store, To feed the bow - els of the poor; To
Or give my bod - y to the flame, To
Or give my bod - y to the flame, To
To
30
gain a mar - tyr's glo - rious name; Be ab - sent, all my hopes are
gain a mar - tyr's glo - rious name; Be ab - sent, all my hopes are
gain a mar - tyr's glo - rious name; Be ab - sent, all my hopes are
gain a mar - tyr's glo - rious name; If love to God, and love to men, Be ab - sent, all my hopes are

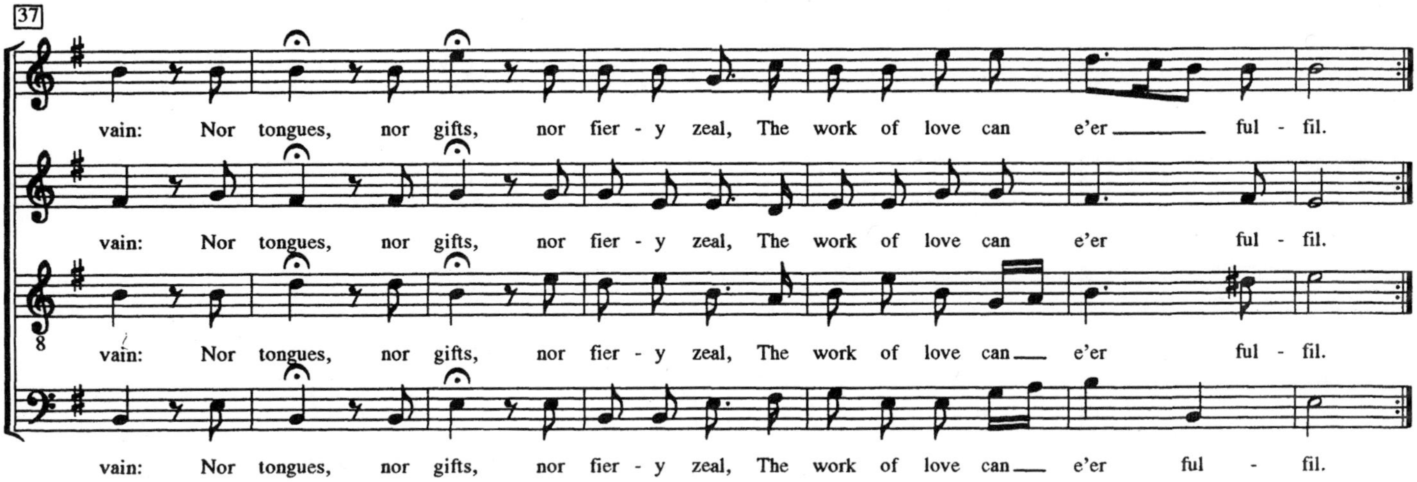

CHINA

Watts Hymns II No.1 **L. M.**

2. Begin to make his glories known,
Ye seraphs, who sit near his throne;
Tune your harps high, and spread the sound
To the creation's utmost bound.

3. All mortal things of meaner frame,
Exert your force, and own his name;
Whilst with our souls, and with our voice,
We sing his honours, and our joys.

4. To him be sacred all we have,
From the young cradle to the grave:
Our lips shall his loud wonders tell,
And ev'ry word a miracle.

5. These western shores, our native land,
Lie safe in the almighty's hand!
Our foes of vict'ry dream in vain,
And wear the captivating chain.

6. Raise monumental praises high
To him, who thunders through the sky,
And, with an awful nod or frown,
Shakes an aspiring tyrant down.

7. Pillars of lasting brass proclaim
The triumphs of th'eternal name;
While trembling nations read from far
The honours of the God of war.

8. Thus let our flaming zeal employ
Our loftiest thoughts, and loudest songs;
Let there be sung, with warmest joy,
Hosanna, from ten thousand tongues.

9. Yet, mighty God, our feeble frame
Attempts in vain to reach thy name;
The strongest notes that angels raise
Faint, in the worship and the praise.

CHINA

CHRISTIAN'S HOPE

Watts Hymns I No.18 **C. M.**

20
kind their slum - bers are! From suff'-ring, and from sin re - leas'd, And freed from
kind their slum - bers are! From suff'-ring, and from sin re - leas'd, And freed from
From suff'-ring, and from sin re - leas'd, And freed from
28
ev' - ry snare. Far from the world of toil and strife, The
ev' - ry snare. Far from the world of toil and strife, They're pres - ent with the Lord; The
ev' - ry snare. Far from the world of toil and strife, They're pres - ent with the Lord;
34
la - bours of their mor - tal life End, end, end in a large re - ward.
la - bours of their mor - tal life End, end, end in a large re - ward.
End, end, end in a large re - ward.

CHRISTMAS

George Richards **C. M.**

35
Piano
harps at - tun'd to love, Thus swept Eph - ra - tah's plain. He comes! he
43
Forte
comes! the sav - iour God: Good will, peace, joy for men. Glad
50
Brisk
tid - ings shout to all a - broad. So be it, Lord, so be it, Lord,
58
Slow
a - men, So be it, Lord, a - men.

CONSECRATION

Watts Horae Lyricae **P. M. [8.8.6.8.8.14]**

2. The dearest nerve about my heart,
Should it refuse to bear a part
With my melodious breath,
I'd tear away the vital chord,
A bloody victim to my Lord,
And live without the impious string,
or show my zeal in death.

CONSECRATION

CRETE

New Version Psalm 120 **P. M. [8.8.8.8.8.8]**

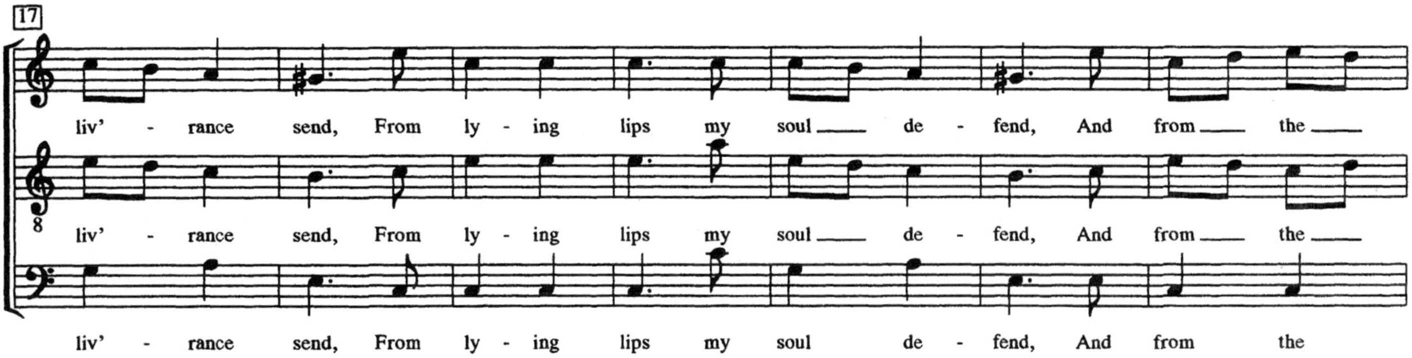

2. What little profit can accrue,
And yet what heavy wrath is due,
O thou perfidious tongue, to thee?
Thy sting upon thyself shall turn;
Of lasting flames that fiercely burn,
The constant fuel thou shalt be.

3. But O! how wretched is my doom,
Who am a sojourner become
In barren Mesech's desert soil!
With Kedar's wicked tents inclos'd,
To lawless savages expos'd,
Who live on nought but theft and spoil.

4. My hapless dwelling is with those
Who peace and amity oppose,
And pleasure take in others' harms:
Sweet peace is all I court and seek;
But when to them of peace I speak,
They straight cry out, "To arms, to arms."

CRETE

CRUCIFIXION

Watts Psalm 22 **L. M.**

2. "This is the man did once pretend
God was his father and his friend;
If God the blessed lov'd him so,
Why doth he fail to help him now?"
Barbarous people! cruel priests!
How they stood round like savage beasts!
Like lions gaping to devour,
When God had left him in their pow'r.

3. They wound his head, his hands, his feet,
Till streams of blood each other meet;
By lot his garments they divide,
And mock the pangs in which he died.
But God his father heard his cry;
Rais'd from the dead, he reigns on high;
The nations learn his righteousness,
And humble sinners taste his grace.

CRUCIFIXION

DELAWARE

Watts Horae Lyricae **C. M.**

15
won, While tune - ful an - gels sound a - broad, The vic - t'ries
won, While tune - ful an - gels sound a - broad, The vic - t'ries
won, While tune - ful an - gels sound a - broad, The vic - t'ries
22
he has won. Now let me rise, and join their song, And
he has won. Now let me rise, and join their song, And
he has won. Now let me rise, and join their song, And
29
Moderato
be an an - gel too; My heart, my hand, my ear, my
be an an - gel too; My heart, my hand, my ear, my
be an an - gel too; My heart, my hand, my ear, my
36
Piano
Forte
tongue, Here's joy - ful work for you, Here's joy - ful work for you.
tongue, Here's joy - ful work for you, Here's joy - ful work for you.
tongue, Here's joy - ful work for you, Here's joy - ful work for you.

2. I would begin the music here,
And so my soul should rise:
Oh for some heav'nly notes to bear
My spirit to the skies!
There, ye that love my saviour, sit,
There I would fain have place
Amongst your thrones, or at your feet,
So I might see his face.

DELAWARE

DISSOLUTION

Watts Hymns II No.28 **C. M.**

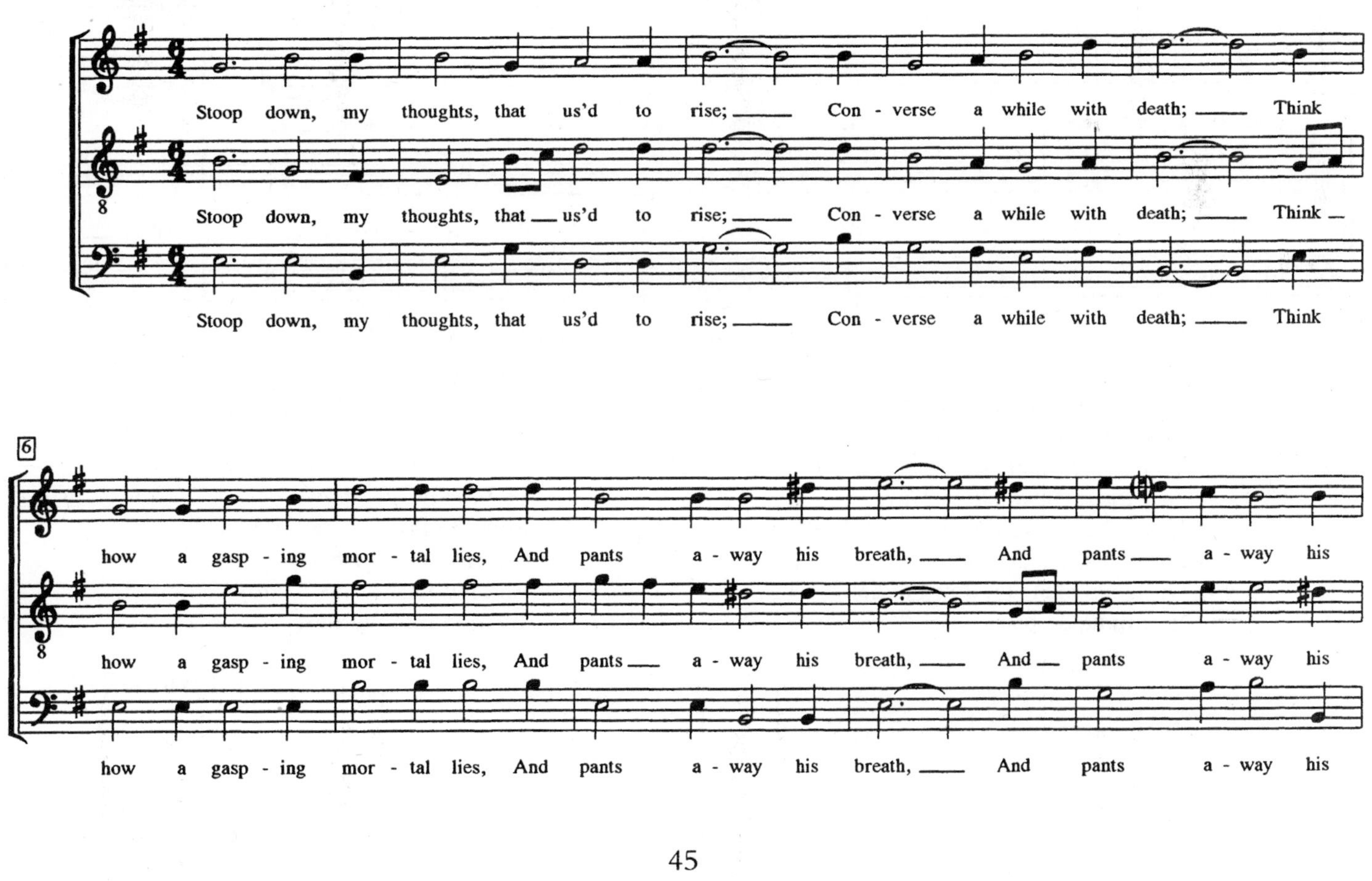

2. But oh, the soul that never dies!
At once it leaves the clay!
Ye thoughts, pursue it where it flies,
And track its wondrous way.
Up to the courts where angels dwell
It mounts, triumphant there:
Or devils plunge it down to hell,
In infinite despair.

3. And must my body faint and die?
And must this soul remove?
Oh, for some guardian angel nigh,
To bear it safe above.
Jesus, to thy dear faithful hand
My naked soul I trust;
And my flesh waits for thy command,
To drop into my dust.

DISSOLUTION

DORCHESTER

Watts Hymns II No.122 **L. M.**

2. Call me away from flesh and sense;
One sovereign word can draw me thence;
I would obey the voice divine,
And all inferiour joys resign.
Be earth with all her scenes withdrawn;
Let noise and vanity be gone:
In secret silence of the mind,
My heav'n, and there my God, I find.

DORCHESTER

DOXOLOGY

Bible, I Timothy 1:17

ELEVATION

Watts Hymns II No.104 **S. M.**

2. Sing how eternal love
Its chief beloved chose;
And bid him raise our ruin'd race,
From their abyss of woes.

3. His hand no thunder bears,
No terror clothes his brow;
No bolts to drive our guilty souls
To fiercer flames below.

4. 'Twas mercy fill'd the throne,
And wrath stood silent by,
When Christ was sent with pardons down,
To rebels doom'd to die.

5. Now, sinners, dry your tears,
Let hopeless sorrow cease;
Bow to the sceptre of his love,
And take the offer'd peace.

6. Lord, we obey thy call;
We lay a humble claim
To the salvation thou hast brought;
And love and praise thy name.

ELEVATION

ELIM

James Merrick **P. M. [7.7.7.7]**

2. Be the Lord your only theme,
Who of gods is God supreme;
He to whom all lords beside
Bow the knee, their faces hide:

3. Who asserts his just command,
By the wonders of his hand;
He whose wisdom, thron'd on high,
Built the mansions of the sky:

4. He who bade the wat'ry deep
In appointed bounds to keep,
And the stars that gild the pole
Through unmeasur'd ether roll.

5. Thee, O sun, whose pow'rful ray
Rules the empire of the day;
You, O moon and stars, whose light
Cheers the darkness of the night.

6. He with food sustains, O earth,
All which claim from thee their birth;
For his blessings wide extend,
And his mercy knows no end.

ELIM

EPHRATAH

Nahum Tate **C. M.**

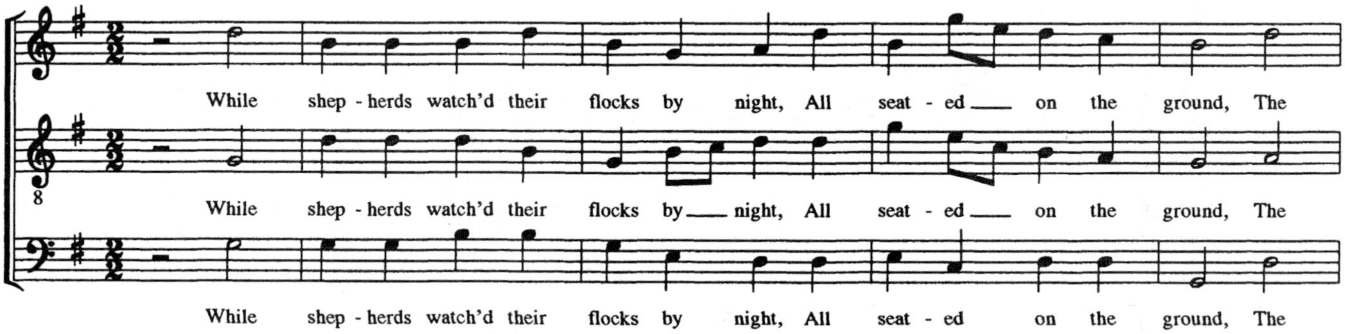

2. "To you in David's town, this day,
Is born of David's line,
The saviour, who is Christ the Lord,
And this shall be the sign:
The heav'nly babe you there shall find,
To human view display'd,
All meanly wrapp'd in swaddling bands,
And in a manger laid."

3. Thus spake the seraph; and forthwith
Appear'd a shining throng
Of angels, praising God, who thus
Address'd their joyful song:
"All glory be to God on high,
And to the earth be peace;
Good will henceforth from heav'n to men,
Begin, and never cease."

EPHRATAH

FLANDERS

New Version Psalm 11 **C. M.**

2. Behold, the wicked bend their bow,
And ready fix their dart,
Lurking in ambush, to destroy
The man of upright heart.

3. When once the firm assurance fails,
Which public faith imparts,
'Tis time for innocence to fly
From such deceitful arts.

4. The Lord hath both a temple here,
And righteous throne above;
Where he surveys the sons of men,
And how their counsels move.

5. If God, the righteous, whom he loves,
For trial, does correct;
What must the sons of violence,
Whom he abhors, expect?

6. Snares, fire, and brimstone, on their heads
Shall in one tempest show'r;
This dreadful mixture his revenge
Into their cup shall pour.

7. The righteous Lord will righteous deeds
With signal favour grace;
And to the upright man disclose
The brightness of his face.

FLANDERS

FLORENCE

Watts Hymns I No.148 **H. M.**

2. At length the Lord, the judge,
His awful throne ascends,
And drives the rebels far
From favourites and friends:
Then shall the saints
Completely prove
The heights and depths
Of all his love.

FLORENCE

GIHON

Watts Psalm 93ii **P. M. [6.6.8.6.6.8]**

2. Upheld by his commands,
The world securely stands,
And skies and stars obey thy word.
Thy throne was fix'd on high,
Before the starry sky:
Eternal is thy kingdom, Lord.

3. In vain the noisy crowd,
Like billows fierce and loud,
Against thine empire rage and roar;
In vain with angry spite
The surly nations fight,
And dash like waves against the shore.

4. Let floods and nations rage,
And all their pow'rs engage,
Let swelling tides assault the sky:
The terrours of thy frown
Shall beat their madness down;
Thy throne forever stands on high.

5. Thy promises are true,
Thy grace is ever new;
There fix'd, thy church shall ne'er remove:
Thy saints, with holy fear,
Shall in thy courts appear,
And sing thine everlasting love.

GIHON

GRATITUDE

Watts Psalm 116ii **C. M.**

2. Among the saints who fill thy house,
My off'ring shall be paid;
There shall my zeal perform the vows,
My soul in anguish made.

3. How much is mercy thy delight,
Thou ever blessed God!
How dear thy servants in thy sight!
How precious is their blood!

4. How happy all thy servants are!
How great thy grace to me!
My life which thou hast made thy care,
Lord, I devote to thee.

5. Now I am thine, forever thine,
Nor shall my purpose move;
Thy hand hath loos'd my bonds of pain,
And bound me with thy love.

6. Here, in thy courts, I leave my vow,
And thy rich grace record;
Witness, ye saints, who hear me now,
If I forsake the Lord.

GRATITUDE

HAMBURG

Watts Horae Lyricae **L. M.**

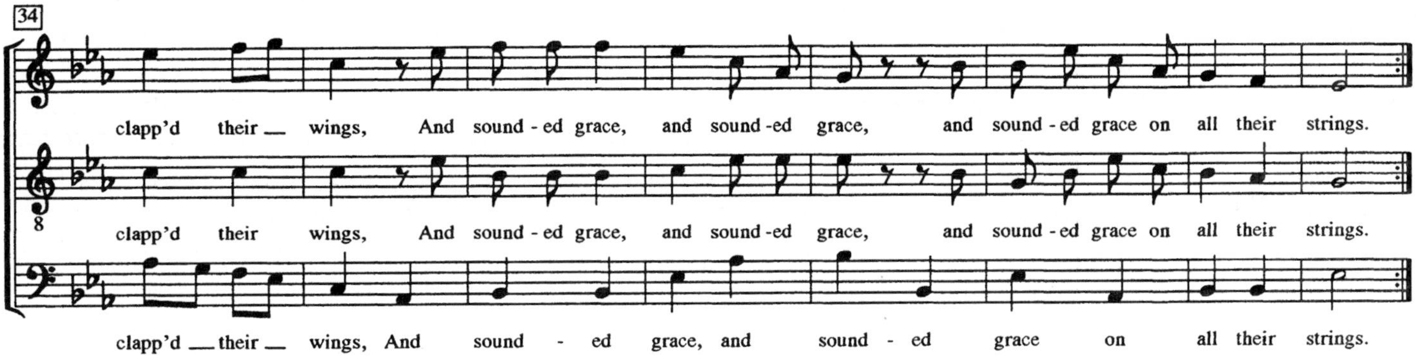

HARVARD

Watts Psalm 147 **P. M. [8.8.8.8.8.8]**

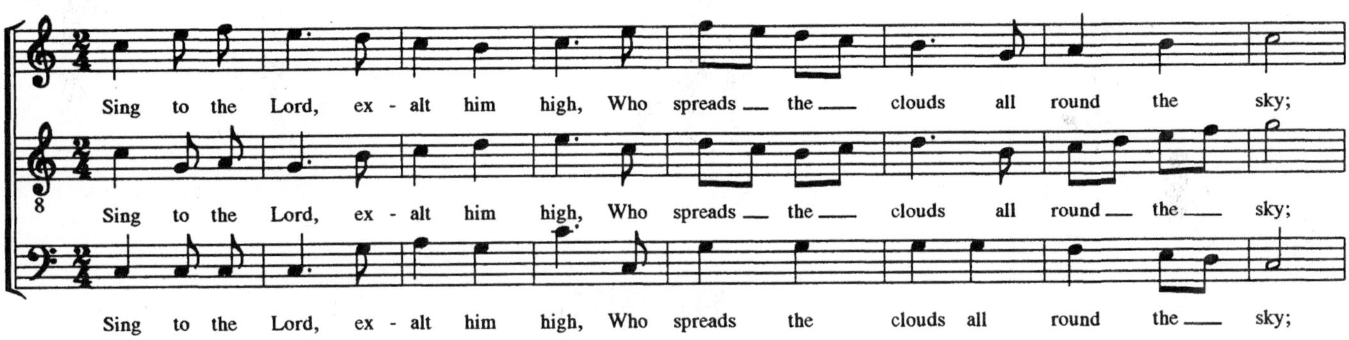

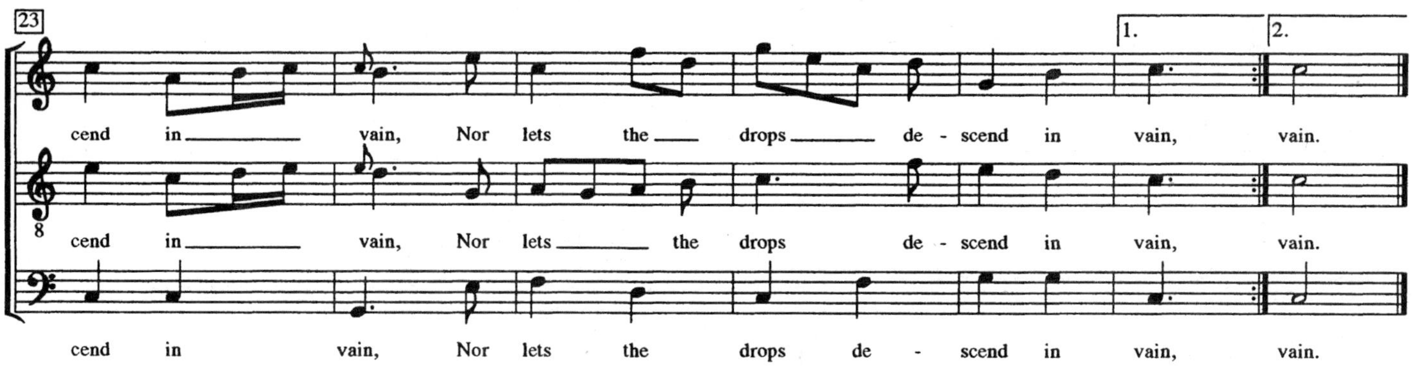

HOREB

Charles Wesley **P. M. [7.7.7.7.7.7]**

2. Yes, our sins have done the deed,
Drove the nails that fix him here,
Crown'd with thorns his sacred head,
Pierc'd him with the soldier's spear,
Made his soul a sacrifice;
For a sinful world he dies.

3. Shall we let him die in vain?
Still to death pursue our God?
Open tear his wounds again,
Trample on his precious blood?
No; with all our sins we part,
Saviour, take my broken heart!

HOREB

HUMILITY

Watts Psalm 39iii **C. M.**

2. Diseases are thy servants, Lord,
They come at thy command;
I'll not attempt a murm'ring word,
Against thy chast'ning hand.

3. Yet may I plead, with humble cries,
Remove thy sharp rebukes;
My strength consumes, my spirit dies,
Through thy repeated strokes.

4. Crush'd as a moth beneath thy hand,
We moulder to the dust;
Our feeble pow'rs can ne'er withstand,
And all our beauty's lost.

5. This mortal life decays apace,
How soon the bubble's broke;
Adam and all his num'rous race
Are vanity and smoke.

6. I'm but a sojourner below,
As all my fathers were;
May I be well prepar'd to go,
When I the summons hear.

7. But if my life be spar'd a while,
Before my last remove,
Thy praise shall be my business still,
And I'll declare thy love.

HUMILITY

IMMANUEL

John Bakewell **P. M. [8.7.8.7]**

2. Paschal lamb, by God appointed,
All our sins on thee were laid;
Great high priest by God anointed,
Thou hast full atonement made!
Contrite sinners are forgiven,
Through the virtue of thy blood:
Open'd is the gate of heaven,
Peace is made with man and God.

3. Jesus hail! enthron'd in glory,
There forever to abide;
All the heav'nly hosts adore thee,
Seated at thy father's side.
There for sinners thou art pleading,
There thou dost our place prepare;
Ever for us interceding,
Till in heaven we appear.

4. Glory, honour, pow'r and blessing,
Thou art worthy to receive;
Loudest praises, without ceasing,
Meet it is for us to give.
Help, ye bright angelic spirits,
Lend your loudest, noblest lays;
Join to sing our saviour's merits,
And to celebrate his praise.

IMMANUEL

INTERCESSION

Watts Horae Lyricae **L. M.**

8
blood, And life, and joys, and crowns a - bove, Dear pur - chas'd
blood, And life, and joys, and crowns a - bove, Dear pur - chas'd
blood, And life, and joys, and crowns a - bove, Dear pur - chas'd
15
by a bleed - ing God. Hark, how he prays, the charm - ing sound Dwells
by a bleed - ing God. Hark, how he prays, the charm - ing sound Dwells
by a bleed - ing God. Hark, how he prays,
22
on his dy - ing lips, For - give, for - give, for - give! And ev' - ry groan
on his dy - ing lips, For - give, for - give, for - give! And ev' - ry groan
For - give, for - give, for - give! And ev' - ry groan
28
and gap - ing wound Cries, fa - ther, fa - ther, let the reb - els live.
and gap - ing wound Cries, fa - ther, fa - ther, let the reb - els live.
and gap - ing wound Cries, fa - ther, fa - ther, let the reb - els live.

LEXINGTON

Philip Doddridge **C. M.**

2. Reduce, O Lord, their wand'ring minds,
Amus'd with airy dreams,
That heav'nly wisdom may dispel,
Their visionary schemes.
With holy caution may they walk,
And be thy word their guide;
Till each, the desert safely pass'd,
On Zion's hill abide.

LEXINGTON

LIMA

Watts Hymns I No.51 **S. M.**

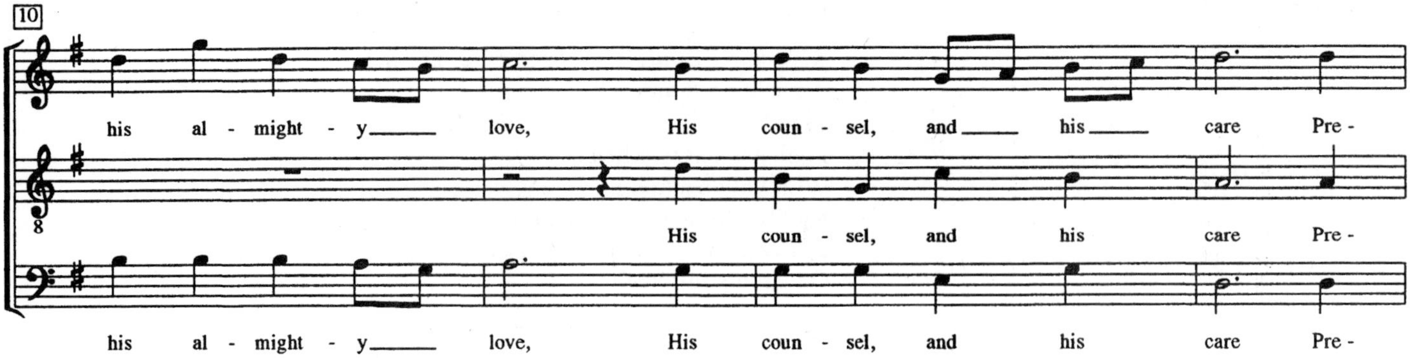

2. He will present our souls,
Unblemish'd and complete,
Before the glory of his face,
With joys divinely great.
Then all the chosen seed
Shall meet around the throne;
Shall bless the conduct of his grace,
And make his wonders known.

LIMA

LUBEC

Watts Hymns III No.9 **S. M.**

2. It cost him cries and tears,
To bring us near to God;
Great was our debt, and he appears,
To make the payment good.
My saviour's pierced side,
Pour'd out a double flood;
By water we are purifi'd,
And pardon'd by the blood.

3. Infinite was our guilt,
But he our priest atones;
On the cold ground his life was spilt,
And offer'd up with groans.
Look up, my soul, to him
Whose death was thy desert;
And humbly view the living stream
Flow from his breaking heart.

4. There, on the cursed tree,
In dying pangs he lies!
Fulfills his father's great decree,
And all our wants supplies.
Thus the redeemer came,
By water and by blood;
And when the spirit speaks the same,
We feel his witness good.

5. While the eternal three
Bear their record above;
Here I believe he died for me,
And seal'd my saviour's love.
Lord cleanse my soul from sin,
Nor let thy grace depart;
Great comforter, abide within,
And witness to my heart.

LUBEC

MEDFORD

Watts Psalm 118 **S. M.**

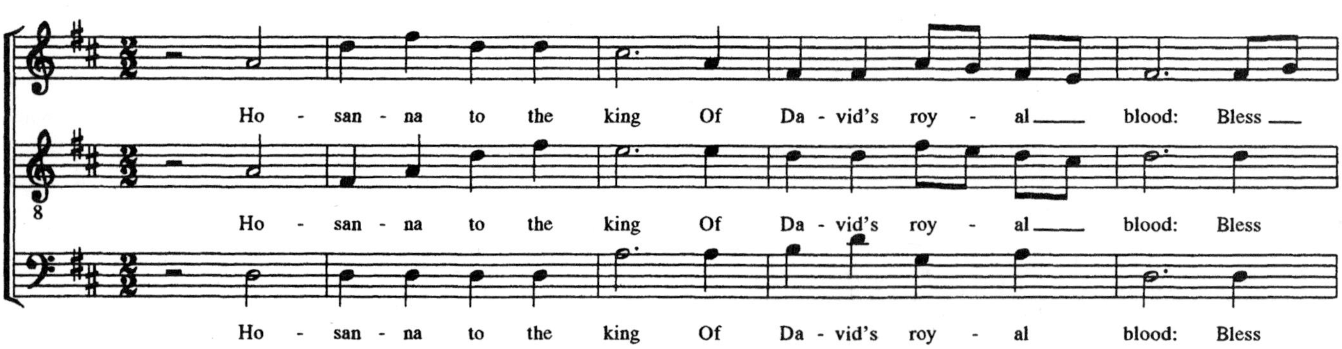

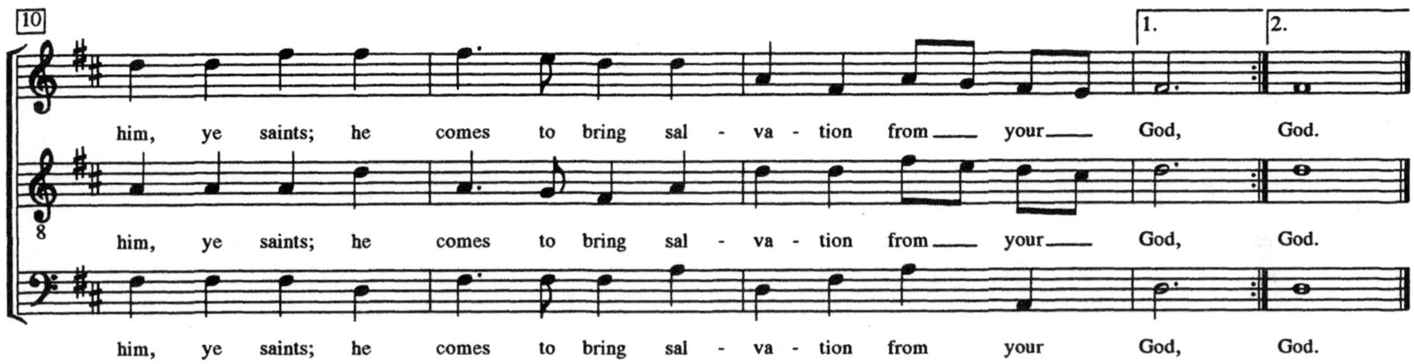

2. We bless thine holy word,
Which all this grace displays
And offer on thine altar, Lord,
Our sacrifice of praise.

MEDFORD

MENOTOMY

Anne Steele **L. M.**

MILTON

Watts Psalm 17 **L. M.**

31
Forte
I shall be near, and like my God! When flesh and sin no more con-
I shall be near, and like my God! When flesh and sin no more con-
I shall be near, and like my God! When flesh and sin no more con-
39
troul The sa - cred pleas - ures of the soul, When flesh and
troul The sa - cred pleas - ures of the soul, When flesh and
troul The sa - cred pleas - ures of the soul, When flesh and
46
1.
2.
sin no more con - troul The sa - cred pleas - ures of the soul, soul.
sin no more con - troul The sa - cred pleas - ures of the soul, soul.
sin no more con - troul The sa - cred pleas - ures of the soul, soul.

MINORCA

P. M. [8.8.6.8.8.6]

2. Thy sov'reign fiat form'd us first,
Thy breath can blow us back to dust,
Frail, sinful, mortal clay;
'Tis thine undoubted right to give
Those earthly blessings we receive,
And thine to take away.

3. All things are under thy control,
Eternal wisdom rules the whole,
Educing good from ill;
Submissive therefore we resign,
Our wills are swallow'd up in thine,
In thy most holy will.

4. In heav'n above, thy will is done;
There, angels wait around thy throne,
Thy counsels to obey;
Adoring at thy feet they fall,
Confess thee sov'reign Lord of all,
And own thy pow'rful sway.

5. Lord, may we join the heav'nly throng,
May mortals learn th'angelic song,
Who dwell beneath the sun;
May ev'ry tongue thy praise proclaim
This be the universal theme,
"Jehovah's will be done."

MORNING HYMN

Watts Hymns II No.6 **C. M.**

2. 'Tis he supports my mortal frame,
My tongue shall speak his praise;
My sins would rouse his wrath to flame,
And yet his wrath delays.
On a poor worm thy pow'r might tread,
And I could ne'er withstand:
Thy justice might have crush'd me dead
But mercy held thy hand.

3. A thousand wretch'd souls are fled,
Since the last setting sun;
And yet thou length'nest out my thread,
And yet my moments run.
Dear God, let all my hours be thine,
Whilst I enjoy the light:
Then shall my sun in smiles decline,
And bring a pleasant night.

MORNING HYMN

NATIVITY

Watts Horae Lyricae **C. M.**

2. Lord! and shall angels have their songs,
And men no tunes to raise?
O may we lose these useless tongues
When they forget to praise!
Glory to God that reigns above,
That pitied us forlorn;
We join to sing our maker's love,
For there's a saviour born.

NATIVITY

NEEDHAM

John Gambold **P. M. [10.11.10.11]**

The time for such tri - fles with me now is o'er; A coun - try I've found where
The time for such tri - fles with me now is o'er; A coun - try I've found where
tri - fles, The time for such tri - fles with me now is o'er; A coun - try I've found where
true joys a - bound, To dwell I'm de - ter - min'd, on that hap - py ground, To
true joys a - bound, To dwell I'm de - ter - min'd, on that hap - py ground, To
true joys a - bound, To dwell I'm de - ter - min'd, on that hap - py ground, To
dwell I'm de - ter - min'd on that hap - py ground, that hap - py ground.
dwell I'm de - ter - min'd on that hap - py ground, that hap - py ground.
dwell I'm de - ter - min'd on that hap - py ground, that hap - py ground.

NEWTON

Philip Doddridge **C. M.**

NORFOLK

Watts Hymns II No.43 **L. M.**

22
Forte
light, And the bright robes he wore___ a - bove; How___ swift and joy - ful
light, And the bright robes he wore a - bove; How swift and joy - ful
light, And the bright robes he wore___ a - bove; How___ swift and joy - ful
light, And the bright robes he wore a - bove; How swift and joy - ful
28
was his flight On wings of ev - er - last - ing love,___ How___ swift and joy - ful
was his flight On wings of ev - er - last - ing love,___ How swift and joy - ful
was his flight On wings of ev - er - last - ing love,___ How swift and joy - ful
was his___ flight On wings of ev - er - last - ing love,___ How swift and joy - ful
33
1.
2.
was his flight On wings of ev - er - last - ing love,___ love!
was his flight On wings of ev - er - last - ing love,___ love!
was___ his flight On wings___ of ev - er - last - ing love,___ love!
was his flight On wings of ev - er - last - ing love,___ love!

2. Down to this base, this sinful earth,
He came, to raise our nature high;
He came, t'atone almighty wrath:
Jesus, the God, was born to die.
Hell and its lions roar'd around;
His precious blood the monsters spilt;
While weighty sorrows press'd him down,
Large as the loads of all our guilt.

3. Deep in the shades of gloomy death,
Th'almighty, captive pris'ner lay;
Th'almighty captive left the earth,
And rose to everlasting day.
Amongst a thousand harps and songs,
Jesus, the God, exalted reigns;
His sacred name fills all their tongues,
And echoes through the heav'nly plains!

NORFOLK

NORTH-KINGSTON

Watts Psalm 95 **C. M.**

2. Let princes hear, let angels know,
How mean their natures seem,
Those gods on high, and gods below,
When once compar'd with him.
Earth, with its caverns dark and deep,
Lies in his spacious hand;
He fix'd the seas what bounds to keep,
And where the hills must stand.

3. Come, and with humble souls adore;
Come, kneel before his face;
Oh may the creatures of his pow'r
Be children of his grace!
Now is the time: he bends his ear,
And waits for your request;
Come, lest he rouse his wrath, and swear,
"Ye shall not see my rest."

NORTH-KINGSTON

OMICRON

John Newton — **P. M. [8.7.8.7.7.7]**

2. Let us love the Lord who bought us,
Pitied us when enemies;
Call'd us by his grace, and taught us,
Gave us ears, and gave us eyes:
He has wash'd us with his blood,
He presents our souls to God.

3. Let us sing though fierce temptations
Threaten hard to bear us down!
For the Lord, our strong salvation,
Holds in view the conqu'rors crown:
He who wash'd us with his blood,
Soon will bring us home to God.

4. Let us wonder, grace and justice,
Join and point to mercy's store;
When through grace in Christ our trust is,
Justice smiles, and asks no more:
He who wash'd us with his blood,
Has secur'd our way to God.

5. Let us praise, and join the chorus
Of the saints, enthron'd on high;
Here they trusted him before us,
Now their praises fill the sky:
"Thou hast wash'd us with thy blood,
Thou art worthy, Lamb of God!"

6. Hark! the name of Jesus, sounded
Loud, from golden harps above!
Lord, we blush, and are confounded,
Faint our praises, cold our love!
Wash our souls and songs with blood,
For by thee we come to God.

OMICRON

PALMER

Watts Psalm 63 **L. M.**

PALMYRA

Watts Hymns III No.7 **L. M.**

16
all ___ my pride. For - bid it, Lord, that I ___ should boast, Save in the death of ___ Christ, ___ my
all my pride. For - bid it, Lord, that I should boast, Save in the death of Christ, ___ my ___
all my pride. For - bid it, Lord, that I should boast, Save in the death of ___ Christ, my
26
God: All the vain things that charm me most, ______ I sac - ri - fice them ___
God: All ___ the vain things that ___ charm me ___ most, ______ I sac - ri - fice ______ them
God: All ___ the vain things that ___ charm ___ me most, I sac - ri - fice them
33
Andante
to ___ his blood, I sac - ri - fice ______ them to his blood. See from his head, his
to his blood, I sac - ri - fice them ___ to ___ his blood. See from his head, his
to his blood, I sac - ri - fice them to his blood. See from his head, his
42
hands, his feet, Sor - row and ___ love flow ___ min - gled ___ down! ______ Did ___ e'er such
hands, his feet, Sor - row and love flow ___ min - gled ___ down! ______ Did ___ e'er such
hands, his feet, Sor - row and love flow min - gled down! ______ Did e'er such

50
love and sor - row meet? Or thorns com - pose so rich a crown? His dy - ing
love and sor - row meet? Or thorns com - pose so rich a crown? His dy - ing
love and sor - row meet? Or thorns com - pose so rich a crown? His dy - ing
59
crim - son, like a robe, Spreads o'er his bod - y on the tree; Then I am dead to
crim - son, like a robe, Spreads o'er his bod - y on the tree; Then I am dead to
crim - son, like a robe, Spreads o'er his bod - y on the tree; Then I am dead to
68
all the globe, And all the globe is dead to me, And all the globe is
all the globe, And all the globe is dead to me, And all the globe is
all the globe, And all the globe is dead to me, And all the globe is
76
1.
2.
dead to me, me. Were the whole realm of na - ture
dead to me, me. Were the whole realm of na - ture
dead to me, me. Were the whole realm of na - ture

84
mine, That were a pres - ent far too small; Love, so a - maz - ing,
mine, That were a pres - ent far too small; Love, so a - maz - ing,
mine, That were a pres - ent far too small; Love, so a - maz - ing,
91
so di - vine, De - mands my soul, my life, my all.
so di - vine, De - mands my soul, my life, my all.
so di - vine, De - mands my soul, my life, my all.

PLACENTIA

John Newton **P. M. [8.8.8.8.8.8.8.8]**

2. His name yields the richest perfume,
And sweeter than music his voice;
His presence disperses my gloom,
And makes all within me rejoice:
I should, were he always thus nigh,
Have nothing to wish or to fear;
No mortal so happy as I,
My summer would last all the year.

3. Content with beholding his face,
My all to his pleasure resign'd;
No changes of season or place,
Would make any change in my mind:
While bless'd with a sense of his love,
A palace a toy would appear;
And prisons would palaces prove,
If Jesus would dwell with me there.

4. Dear Lord, if indeed I am thine,
If thou art my sun and my song;
Say, why do I languish and pine,
And why are my winters so long?
O drive these dark clouds from my sky,
Thy soul-cheering presence restore;
Or take me unto thee on high,
Where winter and clouds are no more.

PLACENTIA

POMFRET

Watts Hymns II No.131 **L. M.**

2. What if we trace the globe around,
And search from Britain to Japan;
There shall be no religion found,
So just to God, so safe for man.

3. In vain the trembling conscience seeks
Some solid ground to rest upon;
With long despair the spirit breaks,
Till we apply to Christ alone.

4. How well thy blessed truths agree!
How wise and holy thy commands!
Thy promises, how firm they be!
How firm our hope and comfort stands!

5. Not the feign'd fields of heath'nish bliss
Could raise such pleasures in the mind;
Nor does the Turkish paradise
Pretend to joys so well refin'd.

6. Should all the forms that men devise
Assault my faith with treach'rous art,
I'd call them vanity and lies,
And bind the gospel to my heart.

POMFRET

PRETORIUM

Watts Hymns II No.95 **C. M.**

18
pain, My dear re - deem - er bore, When knot - ty whips, and rag - ged thorns, His
pain, My dear re - deem - er bore, When knot - ty whips, and rag - ged thorns, His
pain, My dear re - deem - er bore, When knot - ty whips, and rag - ged thorns, His
27
sa - cred bod - y tore, When knot - ty whips, and rag - ged thorns, His sa - cred bod - y
sa - cred bod - y tore, When knot - ty whips, and rag - ged thorns, His sa - cred bod - y
sac - red bod - y tore, When knot - ty whips, and rag - ged thorns, His sa - cred bod - y
36
tore. But knot - ty whips, and rag - ged thorns, In vain do I ac - cuse;
tore. But knot - ty whips, and rag - ged thorns, In vain do I ac - cuse;
tore. But knot - ty whips, and rag - ged thorns, In vain do I ac - cuse;
45
In vain I blame the Ro - man bands, And more the spite - ful Jews. 'Twas you, my
In vain I blame the Ro - man bands, And more the spite - ful Jews. 'Twas you, my
In vain I blame the Ro - man bands, And more the spite - ful Jews. 'Twas you, my

55
sins, my cru - el sins, His chief tor - men - tors were; Each of my crimes be -
sins, my cru - el sins, His chief tor - men - tors were; Each of my crimes be -
sins, my cru - el sins, His chief tor - men - tors were; Each of my crimes be -
63
came a nail, And un - be - lief the spear. 'Twas you that pull'd the venge - ance down Up -
came a nail, And un - be - lief the spear. 'Twas you that pull'd the venge - ance down Up -
came a nail, And un - be - lief the spear. 'Twas you that pull'd the venge - ance down Up -
72
on his guilt - less head: Break, break, my heart, O, burst, mine eyes, And let my sor - rows bleed, And
on his guilt - less head: Break, break, my heart, O, burst, mine eyes, And let my sor - rows bleed, And
on his guilt - less head: Break, break, my heart, O, burst, mine eyes, And let my sor - rows,
81
Slow
let my sor - rows bleed. Strike, might - y grace, my flint - y soul, Till melt - ing wa - ters
let my sor - rows bleed. Strike, might - y grace, my flint - y soul, Till melt - ing wa - ters
let my sor - rows bleed. Strike, might - y grace, my flint - y soul, Till melt - ing wa - ters

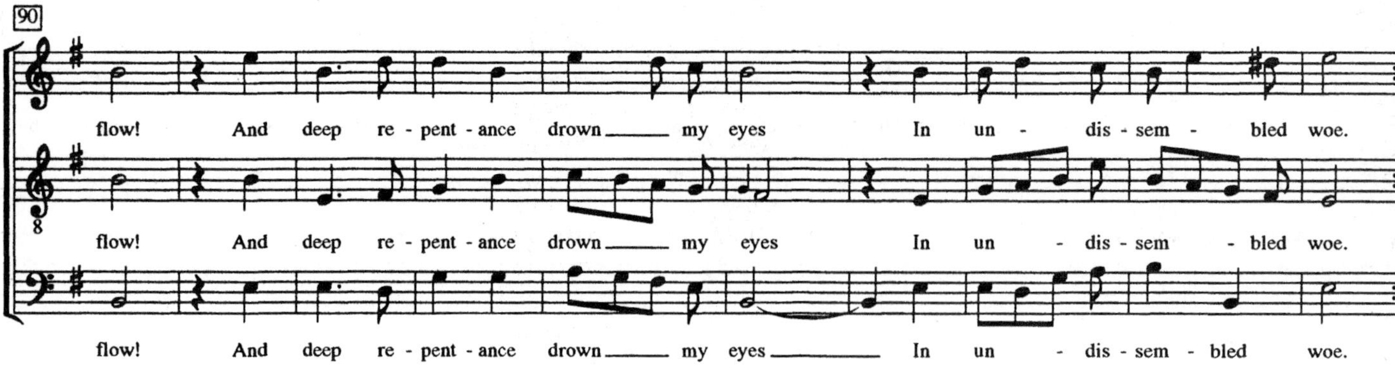

QUINCY

Watts Psalm 50ii **P. M. [10.10.10.10.11.11]**

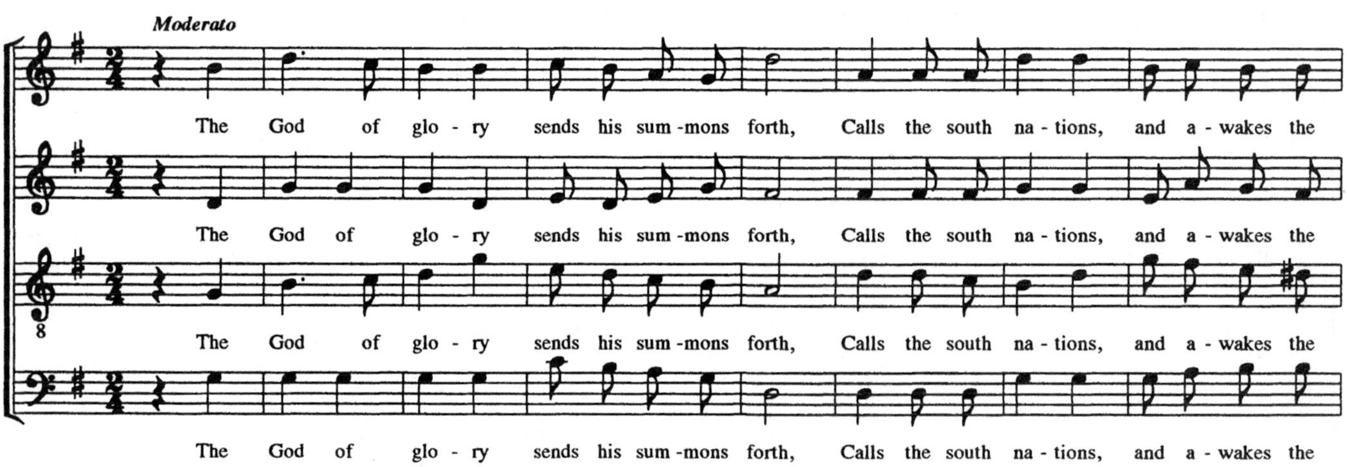

9
north; From east to west the sov' - reign or - ders spread, Through dis - tant worlds, and
north; From east to west the sov' - reign or - ders spread, Through dis - tant worlds, and
north; From east to west the sov' - reign or - ders spread, Through dis - tant worlds, and
north; From east to west the sov' - reign or - ders spread, Through dis - tant worlds, and
17
re - gions of the dead. The trum - pet sounds; Hell trem - bles; heav'n re -
re - gions of the dead. The trum - pet sounds; Hell trem - bles; heav'n re -
re - gions of the dead. The trum - pet sounds; Hell trem - bles; heav'n re -
re - gions of the dead. The trum - pet sounds; Hell trem - bles; heav'n re -
25
joic - es: Lift up your heads, ye saints, with cheer - ful voic - es.
joic - es: Lift up your heads, ye saints, with cheer - ful voic - es.
joic - es: Lift up your heads, ye saints, with cheer - ful voic - es.
joic - es: Lift up your heads, ye saints, with cheer - ful voic - es.

2. No more shall ath'ists mock his long delay;
His vengeance sleeps no more; behold the day:
Behold the judge descend; his guards are nigh;
Tempests and fire attend him down the sky.
When God appears, all nature shall adore him;
While sinners tremble, saints rejoice before him.

3. "Heav'n, earth, and hell draw near: let all things come,
To hear my justice, and the sinner's doom!
But gather first my saints," the judge commands;
"Bring them, ye angels, from their distant lands."
When Christ returns, wake every cheerful passion;
And shout, ye saints; he comes for your salvation.

4. "Behold, my cov'nant stands forever good,
Seal'd by th'eternal sacrifice in blood,
And sign'd with all their names; the Greek, the Jew,
Who paid the ancient worship, or the new."
There's no distinction here; join all your voices,
And raise your heads, ye saints; for heav'n rejoices.

5. "Here," saith the Lord, "ye angels, spread their thrones,
And near me seat my fav'rites and my sons:
Come, my redeem'd, possess the joys prepar'd
Ere time began; 'tis your divine reward."
When Christ returns, wake ev'ry cheerful passion;
And shout, ye saints; he comes for your salvation.

6. "I am the saviour, I th'almighty God;
I am the judge: ye heav'ns, proclaim abroad
My just eternal sentence, and declare
Those awful truths, that sinners dread to hear."
When God appears, all nature shall adore him,
While sinners tremble, saints rejoice before him.

7. "Stand forth, thou bold blasphemer, and profane,
Now feel my wrath, nor call my threat'nings vain:
Thou hypocrite, once dress'd in saint's attire;
I doom the painted hypocrite to fire."
Judgement proceeds; hell trembles; heav'n rejoices:
Lift up your heads, ye saints, with cheerful voices.

8. "Not for the want of goats or bullocks slain,
Do I condemn thee; bulls and goats are vain,
Without the flames of love: in vain the store
Of brutal off'rings, that were mine before."
Earth is the Lord's: all nature shall adore him:
While sinners tremble, saints rejoice before him.

9. "If I were hungry, would I ask thee food?
When did I thirst, or drink thy bullock's blood?
Mine are the tamer beasts, and savage breed,
Flocks, herds, and fields, and forests where they feed,"
All is the Lord's; he rules the wide creation:
Gives sinners vengeance, and the saints salvation.

10. "Can I be flatter'd with thy cringing bows,
Thy solemn chatt'rings and fantastic vows?
Are my eyes charm'd thy vestments to behold;
Glaring in gems, and gay in woven gold?"
God is the judge of hearts; no fair disguises
Can screen the guilty, when his vengeance rises.

11. "Unthinking wretch! how couldst thou hope to please
A God, a spirit, with such toys as these?
While, with my grace and statutes on thy tongue,
Thou lov'st deceit, and dost thy brother wrong."
Judgment proceeds; hell trembles; heav'n rejoices:
Lift up your heads, ye saints, with cheerful voices.

12. "In vain to pious forms thy zeal pretends,
Thieves and adult'rers are thy chosen friends:
While the false flatt'rer at my altar waits,
His harden'd soul divine instruction hates."
God is the judge of hearts: no fair disguises
Can screen the guilty, when his vengeance rises.

13. "Silent I waited, with long suff'ring love:
But didst thou hope that I should ne'er reprove?
And cherish such an impious thought within,
That the all-holy would indulge thy sin?"
See, God appears! all nature joins t'adore him:
Judgment proceeds, and sinners fall before him.

14. "Behold my terrours now: my thunders roll,
And thy own crimes affright thy guilty soul:
Now like a lion shall my vengeance tear
Thy bleeding heart, and no deliv'rer near."
Judgment concludes; hell trembles! heav'n rejoices:
Lift up your heads, ye saints, with cheerful voices.

15. Sinners, awake betimes; ye fools, be wise!
Awake, before this dreadful morning rise.
Change your vain thoughts, your crooked works amend,
Fly to the saviour, make the judge your friend.
Then join, ye saints; wake every cheerful passion:
When Christ returns, he comes for your salvation.

QUINCY

RAMA

L. M.

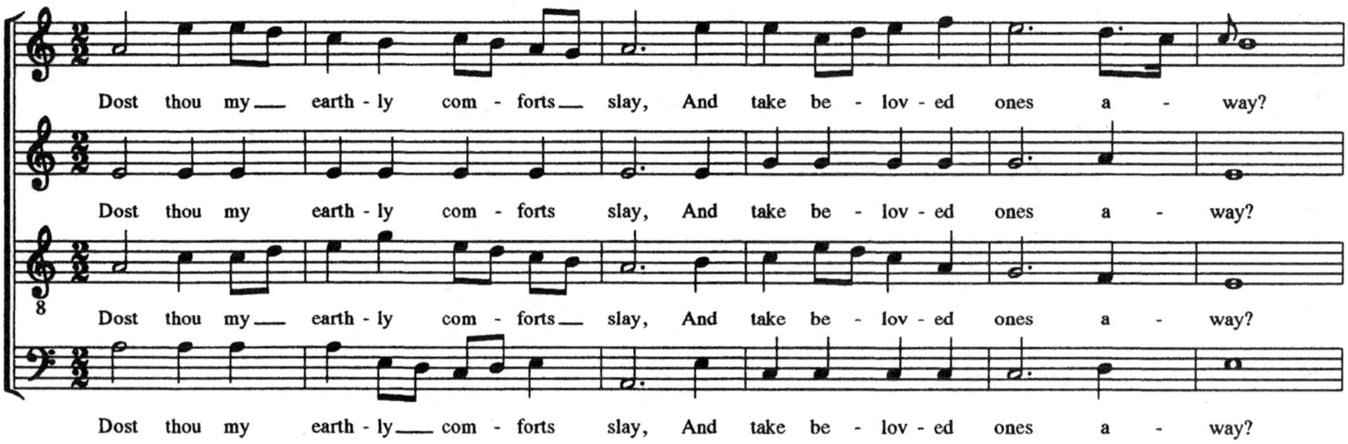
Dost thou my earth-ly com-forts slay, And take be-lov-ed ones a-way?
Dost thou my earth-ly com-forts slay, And take be-lov-ed ones a-way?
Dost thou my earth-ly com-forts slay, And take be-lov-ed ones a-way?
Dost thou my earth-ly com-forts slay, And take be-lov-ed ones a-way?

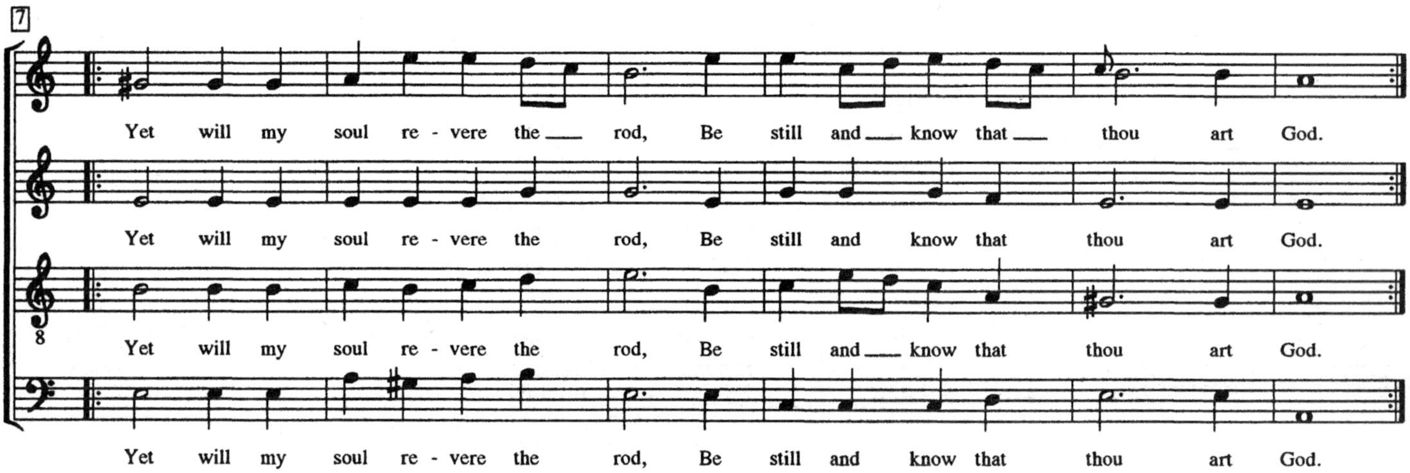
7
Yet will my soul re-vere the rod, Be still and know that thou art God.
Yet will my soul re-vere the rod, Be still and know that thou art God.
Yet will my soul re-vere the rod, Be still and know that thou art God.
Yet will my soul re-vere the rod, Be still and know that thou art God.

RANDOLPH

Watts Psalm 148 **P. M. [8.8.8.8.8.8]**

2. The Lord, how absolute he reigns!
Let ev'ry angel bend the knee:
Sing of his love in heav'nly strains;
And speak how fierce his terrours be.

3. High on a throne his glories dwell,
And awful throne of shining bliss;
Fly through the world, O sun, and tell
How dark thy beams compar'd to his.

4. Awake, ye tempests, and his fame,
In sounds of dreadful praise declare;
And the sweet whisper of his name,
Fill ev'ry gentler breeze of air.

5. Let clouds, and winds, and waves agree
To join their praise with blazing fire;
Let the firm earth, and rolling sea,
In this eternal song conspire.

6. Ye flow'ry plains, proclaim his skill;
Valleys lie low before his eye;
And let his praise, from ev'ry hill,
Rise tuneful to the neighb'ring sky.

7. Ye stubborn oaks, and stately pines,
Bend your high branches, and adore;
Praise him, ye beasts, in diff'rent strains;
The lamb must bleat, the lion roar.

8. Birds, ye must make his praise your theme;
Nature demands a song from you;
While the dumb fish, that cut the stream,
Leap up, and mean his praises too.

9. Mortals, can you refrain your tongue,
When nature all around you sings;
Oh for a shout, from old and young,
From humble swains, and lofty kings.

10. Wide as his vast dominion lies
Make the creator's name be known:
Loud as his thunder shout his praise,
And sound it lofty as his throne.

11. Jehovah, 'tis a glorious word
O may it dwell on ev'ry tongue!
But saints, who best have known the Lord,
Are bound to raise the noblest song.

12. Speak of the wonders of that love,
Which Gabriel plays on ev'ry chord!
From all below and all above,
Loud hallelujahs to the Lord.

RANDOLPH

RESIGNATION

Samuel Wesley, Sr. **C. M.**

7
How vast the love that him in - clin'd To bleed and die for thee!
To bleed and die for thee!
How vast the love that him in - clin'd To bleed and die for thee!
13
'Tis done, 'tis done! the pre - cious ransom's paid; Re - ceive my soul, he
'Tis done, 'tis done! the pre - cious ran - som's paid; Re - ceive my soul, he
'Tis done, 'tis done! the pre - cious ran - som's paid; Re - ceive my soul, he
20
cries: See where he bows his sa - cred head! He bows his
cries: See where he bows his sa - cred head! He bows his
cries: See where he bows his sa - cred head! He bows his
27
1. 2.
head, He bows his head, He bows his head and dies, dies.
head, He bows his head, He bows his head and dies, dies.
head, He bows his head, He bows his head and dies, dies.

RESOLUTION

Watts Psalm 55 **S. M.**

2. My thoughts address his throne,
When morning brings the light;
I seek his blessings ev'ry noon,
And pay my vows at night.

3. Thou wilt regard my cries,
O my eternal God:
While sinners perish in surprise,
Beneath thine angry rod.

4. Because they dwell at ease,
And no sad changes feel,
They neither fear, nor trust thy name,
Nor learn to do thy will.

5. But I, with all my cares,
Will lean upon the Lord;
I'll cast my burdens on his arm,
And rest upon his word.

6. His arm shall well sustain
The children of his love:
The ground on which their safety stands
No earthly pow'r can move.

ROXBURY

P. M. [6.6.6.6.8.8]

SABBATH

Philip Doddridge **L. M.**

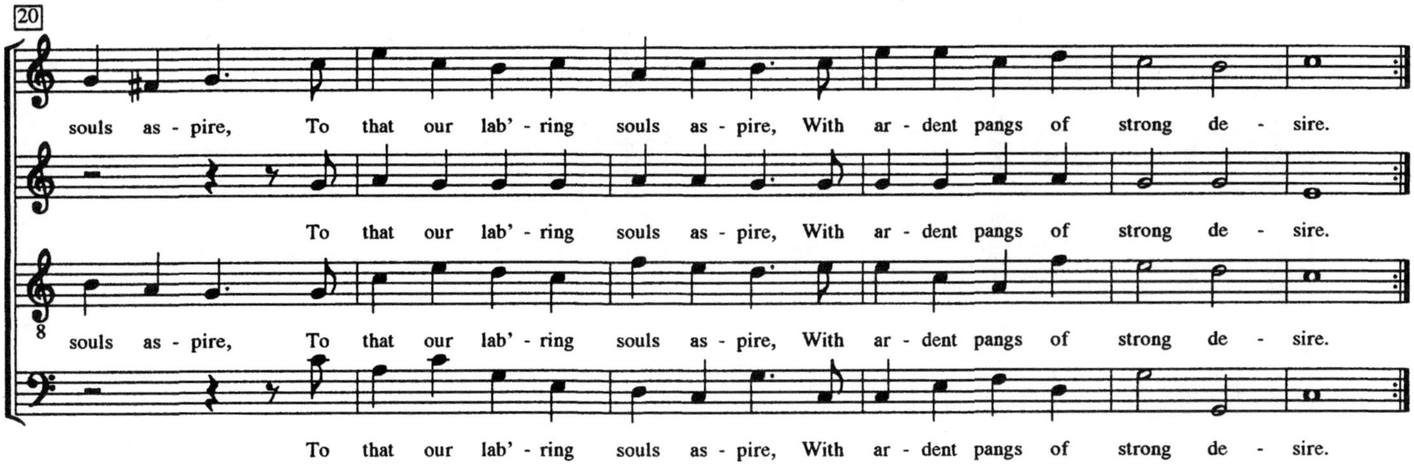

2. No more fatigue, no more distress,
Nor sin, nor death, shall reach the place;
No groans shall mingle with the songs,
Which warble from immortal tongues.
O long expected day, begin!
Dawn on these realms of death and sin;
Fain would we quit this weary road,
And sleep in death, to rest with God.

SABBATH

SMYRNA

Watts Hymns II No.50 **L. M.**

33
Lively
down. Yet why, my soul, why these com - plaints? Still, while he frowns, his bow - els
down. Yet why, my soul, why these com - plaints? Still, while he frowns, his bow - els
down. Yet why, my soul, why these com - plaints? Still, while he frowns, his bow - els
42
move: Still on his heart he bears his saints, And feels their sor - rows and his love.
move: Still on his heart he bears his saints, And feels their sor - rows and his love.
move: Still on his heart he bears his saints, And feels their sor - rows and his love.

SONG

for the Anniversary of St. John the Baptist,
June 24, 5802 [i.e., 1802]

Thaddeus Mason Harris **P. M. [11.12.11.12.12.12]**

2. Saint John was the herald to Jesus the Lord,
And thrice he announc'd, as his blest proclamation,
That from heav'n descends the ineffable word,
The source of all freedom and hope and salvation.
Sure the father of light then reflected his grace on
His messenger Saint John, the first Christian Mason.

3. And O were our wishes of mighty avail,
In regard to the age and the prospect before us!
We would pray that religion and peace might prevail,
And that through the whole world were repeated this chorus:
Unite in expressions of joy and of praise on
The festival day of the first Christian Mason.

SONG FOR . . . ST. JOHN THE BAPTIST

SPRING

P. M. [8.8.8.8]

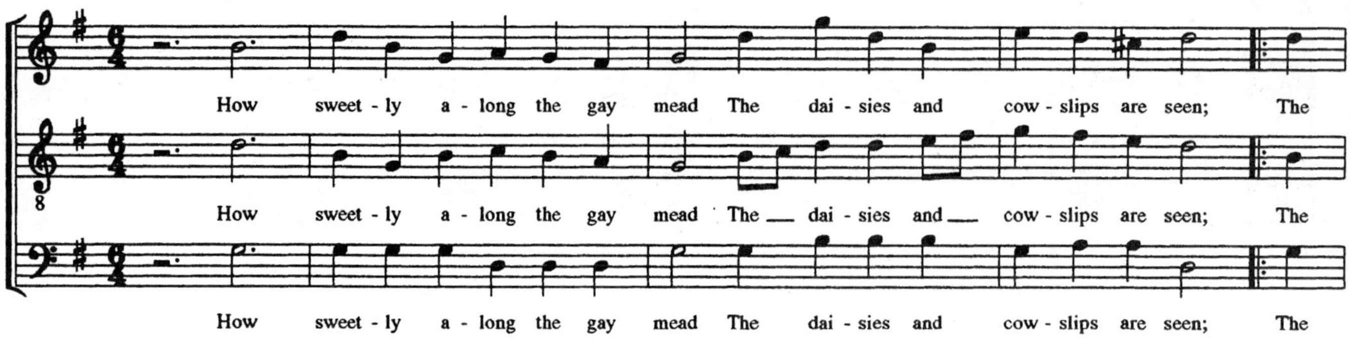

2. The vines that encircle the bow'rs,
The herbage that springs from the sod,
Trees, plants, cooling fruits and sweet flow'rs,
All rise to the praise of my God.

3. Shall man, the great master of all,
The only insensible prove?
Forbid it, fair gratitude's call,
Forbid it, devotion and love.

4. The Lord, who such wonders can raise,
And still can destroy with a nod,
My lips shall incessantly praise,
My soul shall rejoice in my God.

SPRING

STOW

John Newton

P. M. [5.5.5.5.6.5.6.5]

2. We may, like the ships,
By tempests be toss'd
On perilous deeps,
But cannot be lost.
Though Satan enrages
The wind and the tide,
The promise engages,
The Lord will provide.

3. His call we obey
Like Abra'm of old,
Not knowing our way,
But faith makes us bold;
For though we are strangers
We have a good guide,
And trust in all dangers,
The Lord will provide.

4. When Satan appears
To stop up our path,
And fill us with fears,
We triumph by faith;
He cannot take from us,
Though oft he has tried,
This heart-cheering promise,
The Lord will provide.

5. He tells us we're weak,
Our hope is in vain,
The good that we seek
We ne'er shall obtain;
But when such suggestions
Our spirits have plied,
This answers all questions,
The Lord will provide.

6. No strength of our own,
Or goodness we claim,
Yet since we have known
The saviour's great name;
In this our strong tower
For safety we hide,
The Lord is our power,
The Lord will provide.

7. When life sinks apace
And death is in view,
This word of his grace
Shall comfort us through:
No fearing or doubting
With Christ on our side,
We hope to die shouting,
The Lord will provide.

STOW

STRATTON

New Version Psalm 34 **C. M.**

2. Their drooping hearts were soon refresh'd,
Who look'd to him for aid;
Desir'd success in ev'ry face
A cheerful air display'd;

3. "Behold (say they), behold the man
Whom providence reliev'd;
So dang'rously with woes beset,
So wondrously retriev'd!"

4. The hosts of God encamp around
The dwellings of the just;
Deliv'rance he affords to all
Who on his succour trust.

5. O! make but trial of his love,
Experience will decide
How blest they are, and only they,
Who in his truth confide.

6. Fear him, ye saints; and you will then
have nothing else to fear:
Make you his service your delight;
He'll make your wants his care.

7. While hungry lions lack their prey,
The Lord will food provide
For such as put their trust in him,
And see their needs supplied.

8. Approach, ye piously dispos'd,
And my instruction hear;
I'll teach you the true discipline
Of his religious fear.

9. Let him who length of life desires,
And prosp'rous days would see,
From sland'ring language keep his tongue,
His lips from falsehood free:

10. The crooked paths of vice decline,
And virtue's ways pursue:
Establish peace, where 'tis begun;
And, where 'tis lost, renew.

11. The Lord from heav'n beholds the just
With favourable eyes;
And, when distress'd, his gracious ear
Is open to their cries:

12. But turns his wrathful look on those
Whom mercy can't reclaim,
To cut them off, and from the earth
Blot out their hated name.

13. Deliv'rance to his saints he gives,
When his relief they crave:
He's nigh to heal the broken heart,
And contrite spirit save.

14. The wicked oft, but still in vain,
Against the just conspire;
For, under their affliction's weight,
He keeps their bones entire.

15. The wicked, from their wicked arts,
Their ruin shall derive;
Whilst righteous men, whom they detest,
Shall them and theirs survive.

16. For God preserves the souls of those
Who on his truth depend:
To them and their posterity
His blessings shall descend.

STRATTON

SUNDAY

New Version Psalm 118 **C. M.**

6
Piano
Forte
Lord, we be - seech thee, save us now, And make us still re - joice.
Lord, we be - seech thee, save us now, And make us still re - joice.
Lord, we be - seech thee, save us now, And make us still re - joice. Then
11
Then op - en wide the tem - ple gates To which the just re -
Then op - en wide the tem - ple gates To which the just re - pair, That
op - en wide the tem - ple gates To which the just re - pair, That I may en - ter
16
1.
2.
pair, That I may en - ter in and praise My great de - liv' - rer there, there.
I may en - ter in and praise My great de - liv' - rer there, there.
in and praise My great de - liv' - rer there, there.

TRIUMPH

Elizabeth Scott **H. M.**

TRURO

New Version Psalm 149 **P. M. [5.5.5.5.6.5.6.5]**

2. Let them his great name
Devoutly adore;
In loud swelling strains
His praises express,
Who graciously opens
His bountiful store,
Their wants to relieve, and
His children to bless.

3. With glory adorn'd,
His people shall sing
To God, who defence
And plenty supplies;
Their loud acclamations
To him their great king,
Through earth shall be sounded,
And reach to the skies.

4. Ye angels above,
His glories who've sung,
In loftiest notes,
Now publish his praise:
We, mortals, delighted,
Would borrow your tongue;
Would join in your numbers,
And chant to your lays.

TRURO

VERNON

Watts Psalm 45i **L. M.**

2. O'er all the sons of human race,
He shines with a superior grace;
Love from his lips divinely flows,
And blessings, all his state compose.

3. Dress thee in arms, most mighty Lord,
Gird on the sharp, victorious sword;
In majesty and glory ride,
With truth and meekness at thy side.

4. Thine anger, like a pointed dart,
Shall pierce thy foes of stubborn heart;
Or words of mercy, kind and sweet,
Shall melt the rebels at thy feet.

5. Thy throne, O God, forever stands,
Grace is the sceptre in thy hands;
Thy laws and works are just and right,
Justice and grace are thy delight.

6. Thy father, God, hath richly shed,
His oil of gladness on thy head;
And with his sacred spirit blest,
His first born son above the rest.

VERNON

VIENNA

New Version Psalm 148 **H. M.**

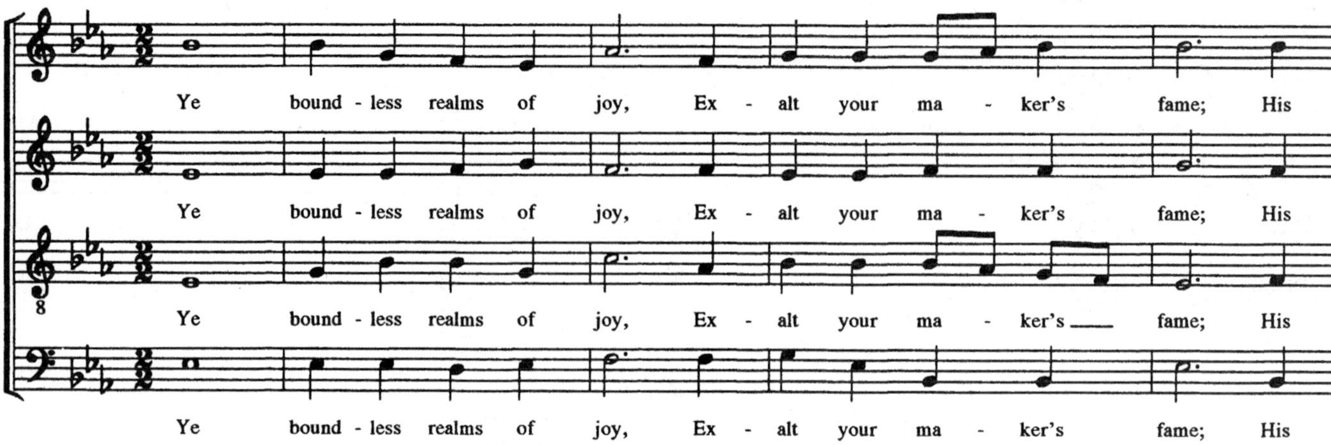

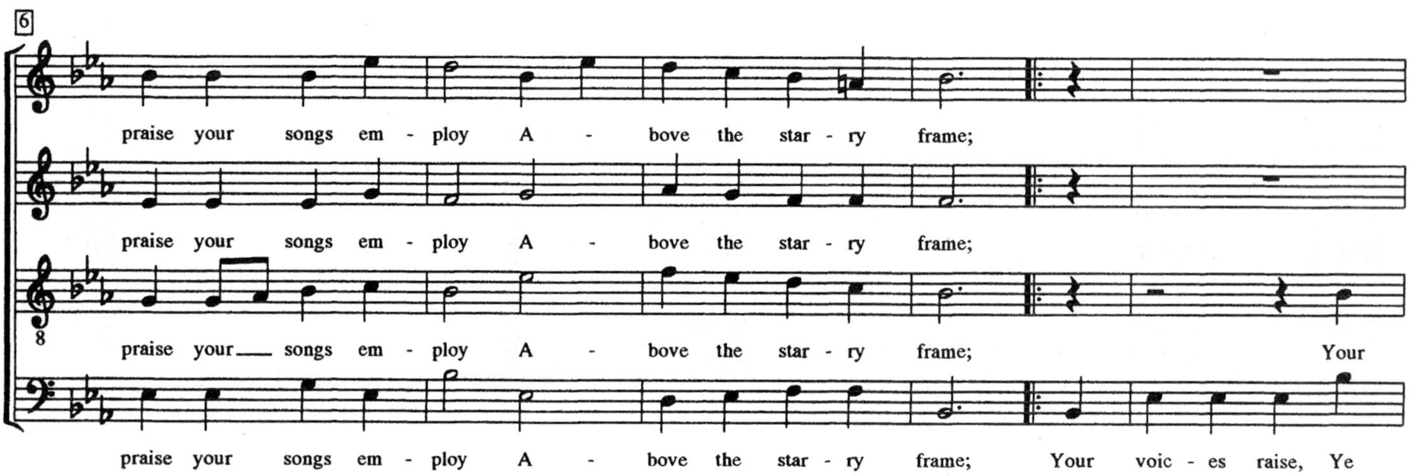

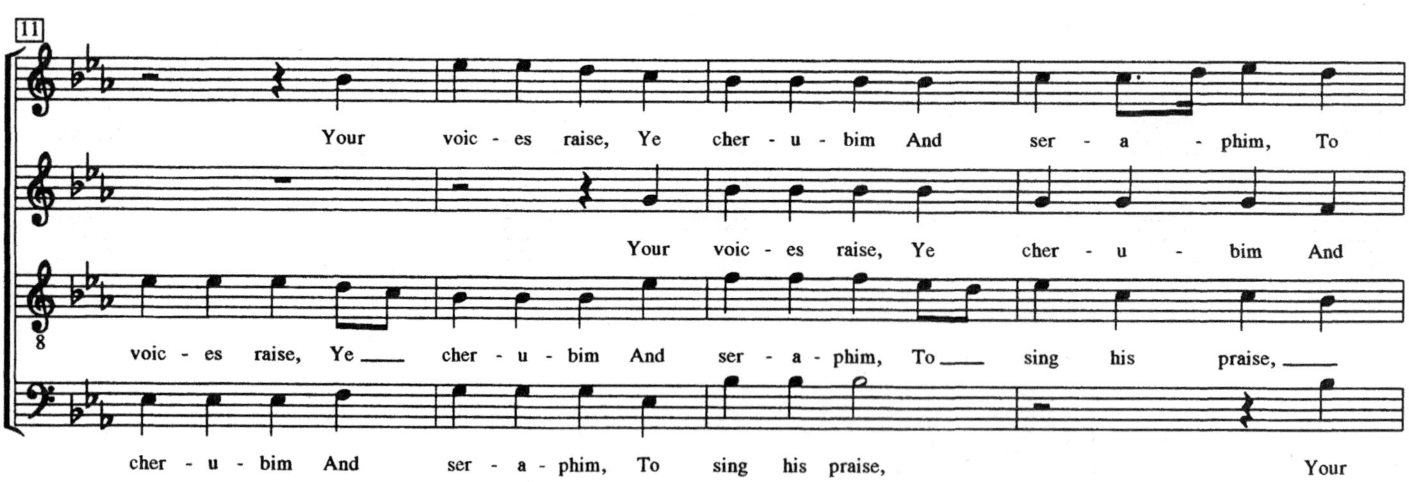

2. Thou moon, that rul'st the night,
And sun that guid'st the day,
Ye glitt'ring stars of light,
To him your homage pay:
His praise declare,
Ye heav'ns above,
And clouds that move
In liquid air.

3. Let them adore the Lord,
And praise his holy name,
By whose almighty word
They all from nothing came:
And all shall last,
From changes free:
His firm decree
Stands ever fast.

4. Let earth her tribute pay;
Praise him, ye dreadful whales,
And fish that through the sea
Glide swift with glitt'ring scales:
Fire, hail, and snow,
And misty air,
And winds that, where
He bids them, blow.

5. By hills and mountains (all
In grateful consort joined)
By cedars stately tall,
And trees for fruit design'd;
By ev'ry beast,
And creeping thing,
And fowl of wing,
His name be blest.

6. Let all of royal birth,
With those of humbler frame,
And judges of the earth,
His matchless praise proclaim.
In this design
Let youths with maids,
And hoary heads
With children join.

7. United zeal be shown,
His wond'rous fame to raise,
Whose glorious name alone
Deserves our endless praise.
Earth's utmost ends
His pow'r obey:
His glorious sway
The sky transcends.

8. His chosen saints to grace,
He sets them up on high,
And favours Isr'el's race,
Who still to him are nigh.
O therefore raise
Your grateful voice,
And still rejoice
The Lord to praise.

VIENNA

WALTHAM

Watts Hymns I No.137 **L. M.**

2. 'Twas his own purpose that begun
To rescue rebels doom'd to die:
He gave us grace in Christ his son,
Before he spread the starry sky.
Jesus, the Lord, appears at last,
And makes his father's counsels known;
Declares the great transactions pass'd,
And brings immortal blessings down.

WALTHAM

WATERTOWN

John Newton **C. M.**

15
Weak is the ef-fort of my heart, And cold my warm-est thought; But
24
when I see thee as thou art, I'll praise thee as I ought, ought.
1.
2.
'Till
32
then I would thy love pro-claim With ev'-ry fleet-ing breath; And may the mu-sic of thy name Re-
Piano
38
fresh my soul in death, And may the mu-sic of thy name Re-fresh my soul in death.
Forte

WESTON

Watts Horae Lyricae **S. M.**

2. The heav'nly dove came down,
And tender'd me his wings,
To mount me upward to a crown,
And bright immortal things.
Lord, I'm asham'd to say
That I refus'd thy dove,
And sent thy spirit griev'd away,
To his own realms of love.

3. Not all thine heav'nly charms,
Nor terrors of thy hand,
Could force me to lay down my arms,
And bow to thy command.
Lord, 'tis against thy face
My sins like arrows rise,
And yet, and yet (O matchless grace!)
Thy thunder silent lies.

4. O shall I never feel
The melting of thy love?
Am I of such hell harden'd steel,
That mercy cannot move?
Now, for one pow'rful glance,
Dear saviour, from thy face!
This rebel heart no more withstands,
But sinks beneath thy grace.

WESTON

WILMINGTON

Watts Hymns I No.5 **C. M.**

2. Peace, all our angry passions, then,
Let each rebellious sigh
Be silent at his sovereign will,
And every murmur die.

3. If smiling mercy crown our lives,
Its praises shall be spread;
And we'll adore the justice too,
That strikes our comforts dead.

WILMINGTON

APPENDIX

Containing Works Attributed to "Babcock"

Whose Authorship is Uncertain

ADMIRATION

Watts Horae Lyricae **L. M.**

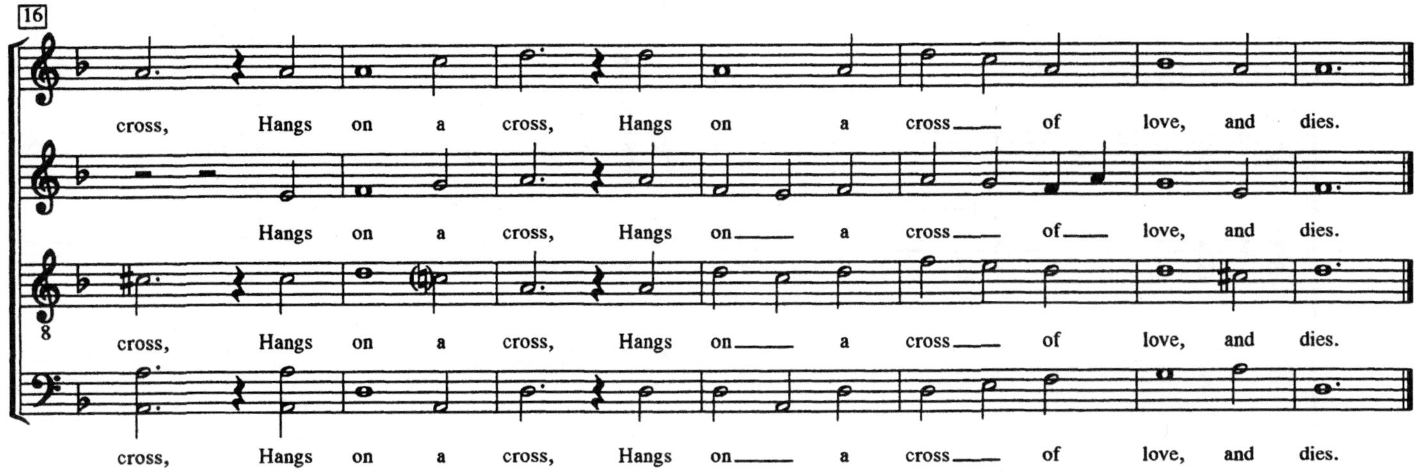

2. Did pity ever stoop so low,
Dress'd in divinity and blood?
Was ever rebel courted so
In groans of an expiring God?

3. Again he lives; and spreads his hands,
Hands that were nail'd to tott'ring smart;
"By these dear wounds," says he; and stands
And prays to clasp me to his heart.

4. Sure I must love; or are my ears
Still deaf, nor will my passion move?
Then let me melt this heart to tears;
This heart shall yield to death or love.

ADMIRATION

SOLITUDE

Watts Horae Lyricae **L. M.**

2. If I behold his bleeding heart,
There love in floods of sorrow reigns,
He triumphs o'er the killing smart,
And buys my pleasure with his pains.

3. Or if I climb th'eternal hills,
Where the dear conqu'rer sits enthron'd,
Still in his heart compassion dwells,
Near the memorials of his wound.

4. How shall a pardon'd rebel show
How much I love my dying God?
Lord, here I banish every foe,
I hate the sins that cost thy blood.

5. I hold no more commerce with hell,
My dearest lusts shall all depart;
But let thine image ever dwell,
Stamp'd as a seal upon my heart.

SOLITUDE

SPRINGFIELD [I]

Charles Wesley **P. M. [7.6.7.6.7.7.8.6]**

7
lone, Tears the graves and moun - tains up By his ex - pir - ing
lone, Tears the graves and moun - tains up By his ex - pir - ing
lone, Tears the graves and moun - tains up By his ex - pir - ing
lone, Tears the graves and moun - tains up By his ex - pir - ing
14
groan: Lo! the pow'rs of heav'n he shakes; Na - ture in con - vul - sion
groan: Lo! the pow'rs of heav'n he shakes; Na - ture in con - vul - sion
groan: Lo! the pow'rs of heav'n he shakes; Na - ture in con - vul - sion
groan: Lo! the pow'rs of heav'n he shakes; Na - ture in con - vul - sion
19
lies, The earth's pro - found - est cen - ter quakes, The great Je - ho - vah dies!
lies, The earth's pro - found - est cen - ter quakes, The great Je - ho - vah dies!
lies, The earth's pro - found - est cen - ter quakes, The great Je - ho - vah dies!
lies, The earth's pro - found - est cen - ter quakes, The great Je - ho - vah dies!

SPRINGFIELD [II]

Charles Wesley **P. M. [7.6.7.6.7.7.8.6]**

WARREN

Thomas Flatman **L. M.**

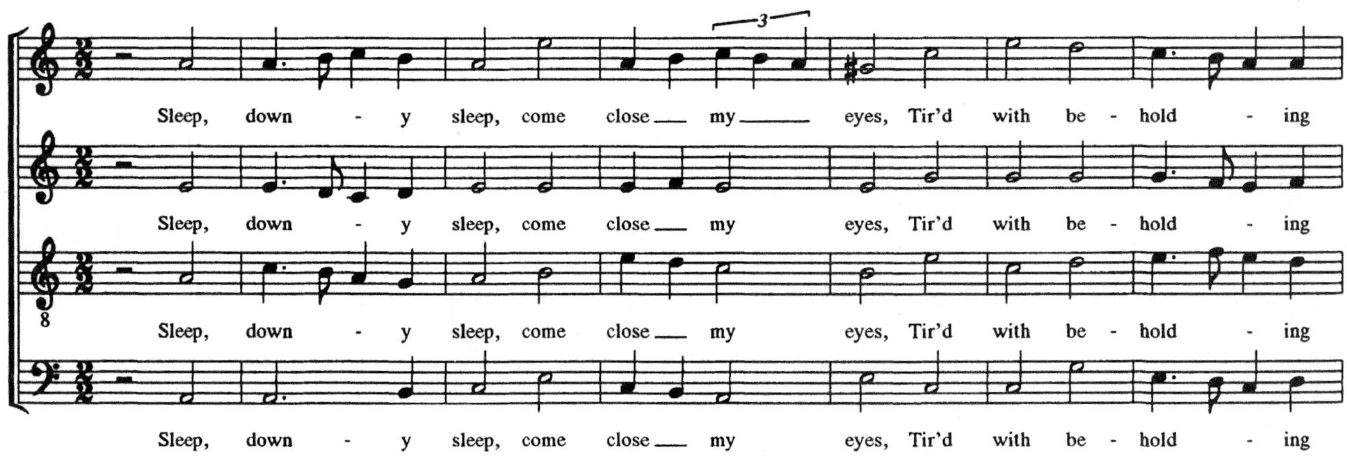

8
van - i - ties: Wel - come, wel-come sweet
van - i - ties: Wel - come, wel-come,
van - i - ties: Wel - come, wel-come, sweet sleep, Wel-come,
van - i - ties: Wel - come, wel-come, sweet sleep, Wel - come, wel-come,
14
sleep, wel-come, wel - come, sweet sleep that driv'st a - way The toils and
sweet sleep, Wel - come, wel-come, sweet sleep that driv'st a - way The toils
wel - come, sweet sleep that driv'st a - way The toils and fol - - lies
wel - come, wel-come, sweet sleep, that driv'st a - way The toils
20
fol - - lies of the day, The toils and fol - - lies of the day.
and fol - lies, The toils and fol - lies of the day.
of the day, The toils and fol - - lies of the day.
and fol - lies, The toils and fol - lies of the day.

WESTBOROUGH

Watts Hymns II No.62 **C. M.**

20
His sound - ing char - iot
His sound - ing char - iot shakes the
char - iot shakes the sky; He makes the clouds his
24
shakes the sky; He makes the clouds his throne; Till
There all his stores of light - ning lie, Till
sky; He makes the clouds his throne; There all his stores of light - ning lie, Till
throne; There all his stores of light - ning lie, Till venge - ance darts them down, Till
29
venge - ance darts them down. What shall the wretch, the sin - ner do? He
venge - ance darts them down. What shall the wretch, the sin - ner do? He
venge - ance darts them down. What shall the wretch, the sin - ner do? He
venge - ance darts them down. What shall the wretch, the sin - ner do? He

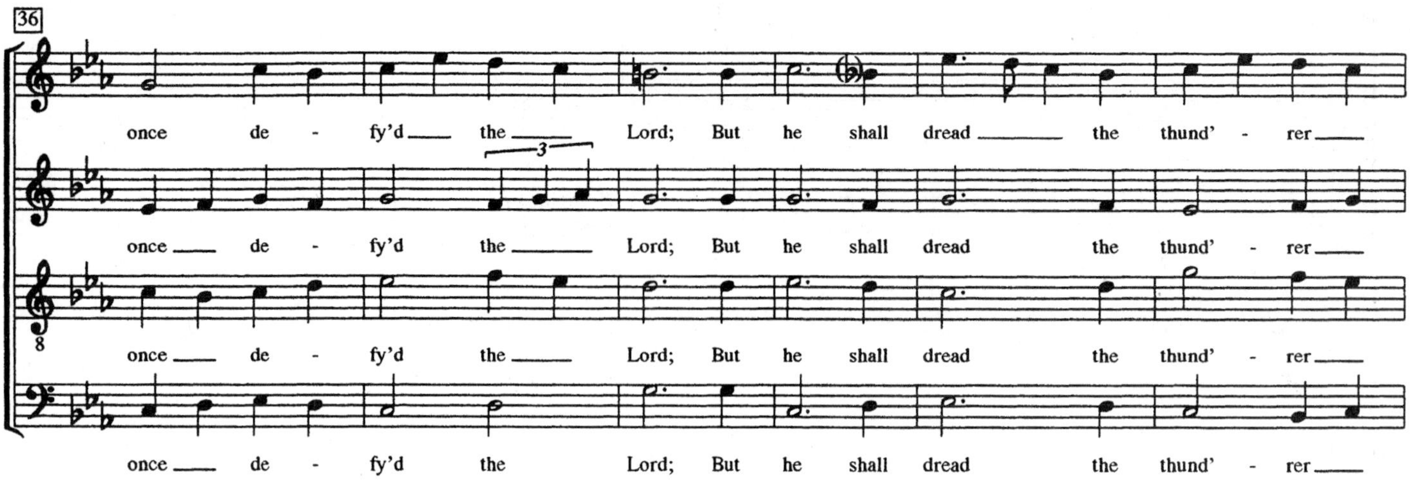
36
once de - fy'd the Lord; But he shall dread the thund' - rer
once de - fy'd the Lord; But he shall dread the thund' - rer
once de - fy'd the Lord; But he shall dread the thund' - rer
once de - fy'd the Lord; But he shall dread the thund' - rer

42
now, And sink be - neath his word.
now, And sink be - neath his word.
now, And sink be - neath his word.
now, And sink be - neath his word.

WRENTHAM

L. M.

Me - thinks I hear the heav'ns re - sound And all the earth ex - alt - ing
ring, To ush - er in this glo - rious day And hail the spot - less in - fant king,
To ush - er in this glo - rious day, And hail the spot - less in - fant king, And
To
To ush - er in this glo - rious day, And

16
To ush - er in this glo - rious day, And
ush - er in this glo - rious day, And hail the spot - less in - fant king, And
hail the spot - less in - fant king, And hail the spot - less in - fant king,
hail the spot - less in - fant king, And hail the spot - less, hail the spot - less, hail the
21
1. 2.
hail the spot - less in - fant king, And hail the spot - less in - fant king, king.
hail the spot - less in - fant king, And hail the spot - less in - fant king, king.
And hail the spot - less in - fant king, king.
spot - less in - fant king, And hail the spot - less in - fant king, king.

Abbreviations and Short Titles

Found in the Commentary

Barbauld, *Poems*	Barbauld, Anna. *Poems*. London: J. Johnson, 1773.
Belknap (1795)	Belknap, Jeremy. *Sacred Poetry: Consisting of Psalms and Hymns*. Boston: J. Belknap, 1795.
Belknap	________. *Sacred Poetry: Consisting of Psalms and Hymns*. Boston: T. Wells, 1820.
Bible	*The Holy Bible, Containing the Old and New Testaments*. Boston: Thomas and Andrews, 1814.
Boston First Universal	*Psalms, Hymns and Spiritual Songs: Selected and Original, Designed for the Use of the Church Universal*. Boston: Thomas and Andrews, 1792.
CH	Stone, Joseph, and Abraham Wood. *The Columbian Harmony*. [Worcester, 1793].
Leavitt, *Seamen's*	Leavitt, Joshua. *Seamen's Devotional Assistant and Mariners' Hymns*. New York: The American Seamen's Friend Society, 1838.
MacKenzie, *Selection*	MacKenzie, John. *A Choice Selection of Psalms, Hymns, and Spiritual Songs*. Woodstock, [Vermont]: D. Watson, 1819.
Methodist Episcopal	*A Collection of Hymns for the Use of the Methodist Episcopal Church*. New York: B. Waugh and T. Mason, 1836.
MH1	Babcock, Samuel. *The Middlesex Harmony: Being an Original Composition of Sacred Music in Three and Four Parts*. Boston: Thomas and Andrews, 1795.
MH2	________. *The Middlesex Harmony: Being an Original Composition of Sacred Music in Three and Four Parts*, 2d ed. Boston: Thomas and Andrews, 1803.
New Version	Brady, Nicholas, and Nahum Tate. *A New Version of the Psalms of David*. London: J. Roberts, 1749.
Newton, *Olney*	Newton, John. *Olney Hymns in Three Books*. London: W. Oliver, 1779. (I, II, and III refer to Books I, II, and III, respectively.)
PA2	Forbush, Abijah. *The Psalmodist's Assistant*, 2d ed. Boston: Manning and Loring, 1806.

Saints' Harp	*The Saints' Harp: A Collection of Hymns and Spiritual Songs for Public and Private Devotion*. Plano, IL: The Reorganized Church of Jesus Christ of Latter Day Saints, 1870.
Select Hymns	Worcester, Samuel. *Select Hymns: The Third Part of Christian Psalmody*, 5th ed. Boston: S. T. Armstrong, 1821.
SH	Law, Andrew. *Select Harmony*. [Cheshire: W. Law?], 1779.
UH	Holden, Oliver. *The Union Harmony, or, Universal Collection of Sacred Music*. Boston: Thomas and Andrews, 1793.
Watts, *Appendix*	Watts, Isaac. *Appendix Containing a Number of Hymns, Taken Chiefly from Dr. Watt's Scriptural Collection*. Boston: J. Edwards, 1762.
Watts, *Horae*	________. *Horae Lyricae: Poems, Chiefly of the Lyric Kind*. New York: E. Duyckinck, 1813.
Watts, *Hymns*	________. *The Psalms, Hymns, and Spiritual Songs of the Rev. Isaac Watts*. Boston: Crocker and Brewster, 1847. (I, II, and III refer to Books I, II, and III, respectively.)
Watts, Psalm	________. *The Psalms, Hymns, and Spiritual Songs of the Rev. Isaac Watts*. Boston: Crocker and Brewster, 1847.
Wesley, *Collection*	Wesley, John. *A Collection of Psalms and Hymns*. Charlestown: L. Timothy, 1737.
Wesley, *Hymns*	Wesley, John, and Charles Wesley. *Hymns on the Lord's Supper*. Bristol: F. Farley, 1745.
Winchell	Winchell, James. *An Arrangement of the Psalms, Hymns, and Spiritual Songs of the Rev. Isaac Watts*. Boston: J. Loring; Gould, Kendall and Lincoln, 1832.

Commentary

This commentary is intended to provide details of the sources of music and text for the edition published here. The user is referred to the Editorial Policy section for criteria applied to the music generally. Listed here for each work are the tune name; any variants in that name found in the sources; the text attribution, if any; the source of the text and any emendations that have been made to the text; the musical source, including important earlier or later printings; any corrections made in the edition that differ from the source; and a Performance Note, calling users' attention to details that need to be considered when performing the work. In both editions of The *Middlesex Harmony* (MH1 and MH2) end repeats were omitted. They have been editorially supplied in this edition.

ADMIRATION

No text att. Watts, *Horae*, "Desiring to Love Christ," stanza 4. Stanzas renumbered to reflect Babcock's choice of text.

CH Not printed by Babcock.

CH differs as follows: m.4, tenor, n.1 is a half note.

ANDOVER

Text att.: Words by Relly. A hymn by John Relly, stanza 1. Text supplied from Boston First Universal, Hymn No. 238.

MH2 Published earlier in MH1.

MH1–2 differ as follows: m.1, bass, key signature has sharp on A.

ANTHEM, Comfort Ye, My People

Orig. title: Anthem. Isaiah, 40th Chap.

Text att.: Isaiah, 40th Chap. Bible, Isaiah 40:1–5 with omissions and alterations; hallelujah chorus added.

MH2 Published earlier in MH1.

MH1–2 differ as follows: m.22, tenor, n.1 lacks dot; m.41, tenor, no first or second endings; m.93, bass, rhythm is eighth, quarter, eighth; m.121, counter, second ending labeled as first ending.

ANTHEM, Lord, Thou Hast Been Our Dwelling Place

Orig. title: Anthem. Psalm 90.

Alternate title in index: Psalm 90th.

Text att.: Psalm 90. Bible, Psalm 90:1–3, 9, 12.

MH2 Published earlier in MH1.

MH1–2 differ as follows: m.49, tenor, n.4 is G natural.

Performance note: m.53, treble, the grace note is an appoggiatura, performed as a quarter note with the following dotted quarter note performed as an eighth note.

ANTHEM, O Come Let Us Sing Unto The Lord

Orig. title: Anthem. Psalm 95, and Other Scriptures.

Alternate title in index: Psalm 95th, and Other Scriptures.

Text att.: Psalm 95, and Other Scriptures. Bible, Psalm 95:1–2, 6–7, Psalm 99:9, and Psalm 100:4 with omissions and alterations; hallelujah chorus added.

MH2 Published earlier in MH1.

MH1–2 differ as follows: m.1, bass, eighth rest; m.19, treble, nn.1–2 are dotted eighth and sixteenth. MH2 differs as follows: m.59, bass, n.2 is an A (corrected in errata).

ANTHEM, Remember Now Thy Creator

Orig. title: Anthem, from Eccl. 12th Chap.

Alternate title in index: Ecclesiastes, 12th Chap.

Text att.: Eccl. 12th Chap. Bible, Ecclesiastes 12:1–5, 7, 13 with omissions and alterations.

MH2

MH2 differs as follows: m.20, counter, tenor, bass, no first or second endings; m.28, counter, tenor, bass, nn.1–2 lack marks of distinction; m.33, bass, half rest; m.54, counter, nn.1–2 are F and E (corrected in errata).

Performance notes: m.28, all parts, the wedge-shaped signs are "Marks of Distinction" and are to be performed as accents, not staccato marks; m.44, counter, tenor, the chromatic clash appears to be intentional.

ASHFORD

No text att. Newton, *Olney* I, No. 58, stanzas 3–5. These are the final stanzas in the hymn.

MH2 Published earlier in MH1.

MH1–2 differ as follows: m.5, Forte placed over n.2; m.19, bass, n.1 is G.

Performance note: m.29, 46, tenor, the grace note is an appoggiatura performed as a quarter note with the following dotted quarter note performed as an eighth note.

AUSPICIOUS MORN

No text att. Barbauld, *Poems*, Hymn No. 3, "For Easter Sunday," stanzas 1, 3. Because of Babcock's unusual text selection, no further stanzas have been supplied. Underlaid text differs as follows: m.21, "on" instead of "in."

PA2 Not printed by Babcock.

Performance note: m.12, treble, tenor, the grace notes are appoggiaturas performed as quarter notes with the following dotted quarter notes performed as eighth notes.

BABEL

No text att. An anonymous hymn printed in *Saints' Harp*, Hymn No. 956, stanza 1. Text source differs as follows: m.7, "swell" instead of "swell'd;" m.8, "While" instead of "When."

MH2 Published earlier in MH1.

CALEDONIA

No text att. Newton, *Olney* I, No. 58, stanza 1. The remaining stanzas of Newton's hymn do not fit Babcock's music, thus no further stanzas are supplied.

MH2 Published earlier in MH1.

MH1–2 differ as follows: m.24, tenor, extra barline between nn.2 and 3.

CAMBRIDGE

No text att. *New Version*, Psalm 100, stanzas 1–4. The entire psalm is set. Since *New Version* numbers stanzas according to biblical verses, stanzas have been renumbered according to poetic meter. Text source differs as follows: m.39, "gate" instead of "gates."

MH2

MH2 differs as follows: m.5, "Loud" placed over m.6; m.9, tenor, bass, n.1 lacks fermata; bass, quarter rest instead of eighth rest; m.13, "Loud" placed over m.14; m.17, tenor, bass, no first or second endings; m.26, tenor, bass, n.1 lacks fermata; m.48, treble, n.2 is a quarter note; m.51, tenor, bass, no first or second endings; m.56, tenor, bass, n.1 lacks fermata; m.60, tenor, n.2 lacks fermata; bass, n.1 lacks fermata; m.72, tenor, bass, no first or second endings.

Performance note: MH2 includes the following note, "N.B. Psalm 97, first part, by Dr. Watts, may be sung in this tune." M.26, treble, tenor, the grace notes are appoggiaturas performed as quarter notes with the following half note performed as quarter notes; m.71, treble, tenor, the grace notes are appoggiaturas performed as quarter notes with the following dotted quarter notes performed as eighth notes.

CANA

No text att. A hymn by Anna Barbauld, stanza 1. Text supplied from Belknap, Hymn No. 216.

MH2

CHARITY

No text att. Watts, *Hymns* I, No. 134, stanzas 1–4. The entire hymn is set.

MH2

MH2 differs as follows: m.33, bass, n.2 is a quarter note (corrected in errata); m.38, 39, counter, tenor, bass, n.1 lacks fermata.

CHINA

Text att.: Words by Dr. Watts. Watts, *Hymns* II, No. 1, stanza 1.

UH Not printed by Babcock.

UH differs as follows: m.1, all parts, half rest lacking.

CHRISTIAN'S HOPE

No text att. Watts, *Hymns* I, No. 18, stanzas 1–3. The entire hymn is set. Text source differs as follows: m.2, "from" instead of "of;" m.9, "savour" instead of "mem'ry;" m.23, "suff'rings" instead of "suff'ring;" m.25, "sins" instead of "sin;" m.30, "this" instead of "the."

MH2

CHRISTMAS

Text att.: Words by Mr. George Richards. A hymn by George Richards, stanzas 4–6. Text supplied from Boston First Universal, Hymn No. 115. These are the final stanzas in the hymn.

MH2 Published earlier in MH1.

MH1–2 differ as follows: m.42, Pia. placed over m.43; m.45, treble, nn.1–3 slurred; m. 49, Forte placed over m.50; m.62, Slow placed over n.2.

Performance note: mm.46–47, all parts, the wedge-shaped signs are "Marks of Distinction" and are to be performed as accents, not staccato marks.

CONSECRATION

No text att. Watts, *Horae*, "Self-consecration," stanza 4. The remaining stanza of Watt's poem does not fit Babcock's music, thus it is not supplied. Text source differs as follows: m.7, "song" instead of "praise;" m.10, "notes" instead of "song."

MH2

MH2 differs as follows: m.1, treble, meter signature is 4/4; m.8, n.2 forte appears in m.10.

Performance note: mm.8, 16, 25, tenor, m.20, treble, the grace notes are appoggiaturas performed as quarter notes with the following dotted quarter note performed as eighth notes.

CRETE

No text att. *New Version*, Psalm 120, stanza 1. Since *New Version* numbers stanzas according to biblical verses, stanzas have been renumbered according to poetic meter.

MH2

MH2 differs as follows: m.23, tenor, n.1 may be A.

Performance note: m.9, tenor, the grace note is an appoggiatura performed as a quarter note with the following dotted quarter note performed as an eighth note.

CRUCIFIXION

No text att. Watts Psalm 22, stanzas 1–2. Stanzas renumbered to reflect Babcock's choice of text.

MH2

DELAWARE

Text att.: Dr. Watt's Lyric Poems. Watts, *Horae*, "The Song of Angels Above," stanzas 18–19. Stanzas renumbered to reflect Babcock's choice of text. Of the three remaining stanzas in the hymn, one will not fit Babcock's music. Stanza 22, as follows, has been omitted:

I am confined to earth no more,
But mount in haste above,
To bless the God that I adore,
And sing the man I love.

MH2 Published earlier in MH1.

MH1–2 differ as follows: m.26, tenor, n.1 dot lacking; m.36, Pia. placed over m.37; m.39, Forte placed over m.40.
Performance note: mm.12, 20, 36, tenor, mm.36, 39, treble, the grace notes are appoggiaturas performed as quarter notes with the following dotted quarter notes performed as eighth notes.

DISSOLUTION

Text att.: Words by Dr. Watts. Watts, *Hymns* II, No. 28, stanzas 1–2. Stanzas renumbered to reflect Babcock's choice of text. Text source differs as follows: m.14, "lip hangs" instead of "lips hang;" m.17, "is" instead of "are."
MH2 Published earlier in MH1.
MH1–2 differ as follows: m.24, "Pia." placed over m.25. MH2 differs as follows: m.1, tenor, n.1 is a half note; m.3, bass, n.1 is a half note.

DORCHESTER

Text att.: Words by Dr. Watts. Watts, *Hymns* II, No. 122, stanzas 1–2. Stanzas renumbered to reflect Babcock's choice of text.
MH2 Published earlier in MH1.
MH1–2 differ as follows: m.21, treble, r.1 is a whole rest.

DOXOLOGY

No text att. Bible, I Timothy 1:17. Text source differs as follows: m.9, "honour" instead of "glory;" m.10, "glory" instead of "honour;" mm. 10–11, "through Jesus Christ" omitted.
MH1

ELEVATION

No text att. Watts, *Hymns* II, No. 104, stanza 1.
MH2
MH2 differs as follows: m.15, treble, second ending, n.1 is D; m.15, tenor, bass, no first or second endings.

ELIM

No text att. James Merrick, Psalm 136, stanza 1. Text supplied from Belknap, Psalm No. 136.
MH2

EPHRATAH

No text att. A hymn by Nahum Tate, stanzas 1–2. Stanzas renumbered to reflect Babcock's choice of text. Text supplied from *Select Hymns*, No. 9.
MH2
MH2 differs as follows: m.1, all parts, rests lacking.

FLANDERS

No text att. *New Version*, Psalm 11, stanza 1.
MH2 Published earlier in MH1.
MH1–2 differ as follows: m.1, bass, key signature has flat on D.

FLORENCE

No text att. Watts, *Hymns* I, No. 148, stanza 6. Stanzas renumbered to reflect Babcock's choice of text.
MH2
Performance note: m.4, treble, tenor, the grace notes are appoggiaturas performed as quarter notes with the following dotted quarter notes performed as eighth notes.

GIHON

No text att. Watts Psalm 93ii, stanza 1.
MH2
MH2 differs as follows: m.1, all parts, half rest lacking; m.15, counter, tenor, bass, no first or second endings.
Performance note: m.10, treble, the grace note is an appoggiatura performed as a half note with the following dotted half note performed as a quarter note.

GRATITUDE

No text att. Watts Psalm 116ii, stanza 1.
MH2
MH2 differs as follows: m.15, tenor, bass, no first or second endings.

HAMBURG

Text Att.: Dr. Watt's Lyric Poems. Watts, *Horae*, "Confession and Pardon," stanza 16. This is the final stanza in the poem. Text source differs as follows: mm.2–3, "says" instead of "saith;" mm:16–17, 20–21, "to wash" instead of "that washed."

MH2 Published earlier in MH1.

Performance note: mm.14, 18, tenor, the grace notes are appoggiaturas performed as quarter notes with the following half note performed as a quarter note.

HARVARD

No text att. Watts Psalm 147, stanza 5 lines 1–3, stanza 6 lines 1–2, stanza 5 line 4. Because of Babcock's unusual text selection, no further stanzas have been supplied.

MH2

MH2 differs as follows: m.28, tenor, bass, no first or second endings.

Performance note: m.24, treble, tenor, the grace notes are appoggiaturas performed as quarter notes with the following dotted quarter note performed as eighth notes.

HOREB

No text att. Wesley, *Hymns* No. 23, stanza 1.

MH2 Published earlier in MH1.

MH1–2 differ as follows: m.18, Forte placed over n.2; m.22, Piano placed over n.2; m.26, Forte placed over n.2; m.30, Mezzo Piano placed over n.2.

HUMILITY

No text att. Watts Psalm 39iii, stanza 1.

MH2

MH2 differs as follows: m.14, tenor, bass, no first or second endings.

Performance note: m.7, treble, m.11, tenor, the grace notes are appoggiaturas performed as quarter notes with the following dotted quarter note performed as eighth notes.

IMMANUEL

No text att. A hymn by John Bakewell, stanzas 1–2. Stanzas renumbered to reflect Babcock's choice of text. Text supplied from Belknap, Hymn No. 93. Text source differs as follows: mm.21–22, "Bearer of" instead of "Thou didst bear;" m.26 "merits" instead of "merit."

MH2

INTERCESSION

Text att.: Dr. Watt's Lyric Poems. Watts, *Horae*, "The Law and Gospel," stanzas 3–4. The remaining stanzas of Watt's poem do not fit Babcock's music, thus no further stanzas are supplied.

MH2 Published earlier in MH1.

Performance note: m.19, all parts, the wedge-shaped signs are "Marks of Distinction" and are to be performed as accents, not staccato marks.

LEXINGTON

No text att. A hymn by Philip Doddridge, stanzas 1–2. Stanzas renumbered to reflect Babcock's choice of text. Text supplied from Watts, *Appendix*, Hymn No. 103.

MH2

MH2 differs as follows: m.1, all parts, half rest lacking; m.17, all parts, n.1 is a dotted half; tenor, bass, no first or second endings.

LIMA

No text att. Watts, *Hymns* I, No. 51, stanzas 1–2. Stanzas renumbered to reflect Babcock's choice of text. Watts's hymn contains a fifth stanzas that does not fit Babcock's music. Stanza 5, as follows, has been omitted:

To our redeemer God
Wisdom with pow'r belongs;
Immortal crowns of majesty,
And everlasting songs.

MH2

MH2 differs as follows: m.1, all parts, half rest lacking; m.17, tenor, bass, no first or second endings.

LUBEC

No text att. Watts, *Hymns* III, No. 9, stanzas 1–2. Stanzas renumbered to reflect Babcock's choice of text. Text source differs as follows: m.9, "fetch" instead of "bring."

MH2

MH2 differs as follows: m.21, tenor, bass, no first or second endings.

MEDFORD

No text att. Watts Psalm 118, stanza 5. Stanzas renumbered to reflect Babcock's choice of text.

MH2

MH2 differs as follows: m.1, all parts, half rest lacking; m.13, tenor, bass, no first or second endings.

MENOTOMY

No text att. A hymn by Anne Steele, stanza 1, stanza 2 lines 1–2, and stanza 3 lines 3–4. Text supplied from Belknap, Hymn No. 258. Because of Babcock's unusual text selection, no further stanzas have been supplied. Text source differs as follows: m.26, "O" instead of "Then."

MH2

MH2 differs as follows: m.1, all parts, rest lacking; m.26 Forte placed over m.27.

Performance note: mm.13, 30, treble, tenor, m.26, treble, the grace notes are appoggiaturas performed as quarter notes with the following dotted quarter notes performed as eighth notes.

MILTON

No text att. Watts Psalm 17, stanza 6 followed by stanza 5. These are the final stanzas in the psalm. Text source differs as follows: m.2, "will" instead of "shall;" m.35, "And" instead of "When."

MH2 Published earlier in MH1.

MH2 differs as follows: m.42, tenor, bass, n.3 is a quarter note (corrected in errata).

Performance note: m.19, treble, tenor, the grace notes are appoggiaturas performed as quarter notes with the following dotted quarter notes performed as eighth notes.

MINORCA

No text att. An anonymous hymn printed in Belknap, Hymn No. 11, stanza 1.

MH2

MH2 differs as follows: m.13, tenor, bass, no first or second endings.

MORNING HYMN

No text att. Watts, *Hymns* II, No. 6, stanzas 1–2. Stanzas renumbered to reflect Babcock's choice of text. Text source differs as follows: m.13, "The" instead of "And." Underlaid text differs as follows: m.8, "that rolls" instead of "who rules."

MH2

MH2 differs as follows: m.1, all parts, half rest lacking.

NATIVITY

No text att. Watts, *Horae*, "Nativity of Christ," stanzas 5–6. Stanzas renumbered to reflect Babcock's choice of text.

MH2

MH2 differs as follows: m.20, tenor, n.2 lacks fermata; bass, n.1 lacks fermata; m. 21, tenor, bass, nn.1–3 lack marks of distinction.

Performance note: m.21 all parts, the wedge-shaped signs are "Marks of Distinction" and are to be performed as accents, not staccato marks.

NEEDHAM

No text att. A hymn by John Gambold, stanza 1. Text supplied from Methodist Episcopal, Hymn No. 260. Because of Babcock's unusual text setting, no further stanzas have been supplied.

MH2 Published earlier in MH1.

NEWTON

Text att.: Words by Dr. Watts. A hymn by Philip Doddridge, stanzas 5–6. These are the final stanzas in the hymn. Text supplied from

Watts, *Appendix,* Hymn No. 100.
MH2 Published earlier in MH1.

NORFOLK

No text att. Watts, *Hymns* II, No. 43, stanzas 1–2. Stanzas renumbered to reflect Babcock's choice of text. Text source differs as follows: m.28, "the" instead of "his." Watts's hymn contains seven stanzas, one of which will not fit Babcock's music. Stanza 6, as follows, has been omitted:

Lift up your eyes, ye sons of light,
Up to this throne of shining grace;
See what immortal glories sit
Round the sweet beauties of his face.

MH2
MH2 differs as follows: m.7, Piano placed over m.8; m.19, Piano placed over n.2; m.26, Forte placed over m.27; m.34, tenor, n.4 is B; bass, n.2 is A; m.36, counter, tenor, bass, no first or second endings.
Performance note: m.7, treble, tenor, the grace notes are appoggiaturas performed as quarter notes with the following dotted quarter notes performed as eighth notes.

NORTH-KINGSTON

No text att. Watts Psalm 95, stanzas 1–2. Stanzas renumbered to reflect Babcock's choice of text. Text source differs as follows: m.19, "sight" instead of "throne;" mm.22–26, "The Lord's a God of boundless might" instead of "The great Jehovah reigns alone."
MH2
Performance note: m.26, tenor, the grace note is an appoggiatura performed as a quarter note with the following dotted quarter note performed as an eighth note.

OMICRON

No text att. Newton, *Olney* III, No. 82, stanza 1. Text source differs as follows: m.6, "the" instead of "our;" m.10, "hush'd" instead of "quell'd;" mm.21–24, "He has brought us nigh to God" instead of "Soon he'll bring us home to God."
MH2 Published earlier in MH1.

PALMER

No text att. Watts Psalm 63, stanza 8. This is the final stanza in the psalm. Text source differs as follows: mm.14–15 "spend the remnant of my" instead of "well employ my future."
MH2
MH2 differs as follows: m.1, all parts, half rest lacking; m.16, tenor, bass, no first or second endings.

PALMYRA

No text att. Watts, *Hymns* III, No. 7, stanzas 1–5. The entire hymn is set. Text source differs as follows: mm.33, 37, "thy" instead of "his;" m.66, "am I" instead of "I am."
MH2 Published earlier in MH1.
MH1–2 differ as follows: m.44, treble, n.1 is C (corrected in errata); m.73, treble, quarter rest instead of eighth rest. MH2 differs as follows: m.68, treble, n.3 is an eighth note (corrected in errata).
Performance note: m.92, treble, tenor, the chromatic clash appears to be intentional.

PLACENTIA

No text att. Newton, *Olney* I, No. 46, stanza 1.
MH2
MH2 differs as follows: m.5, tenor, n.2 lacks fermata; bass, r.2 lacks fermata; m.12, treble, fermata over rest; tenor, n.5 lacks fermata; bass, n.4 lacks fermata; m.16, tenor, bass, no first or second endings.

POMFRET

No text att. Watts, *Hymns* II, No. 131, stanza 1.
MH2 Published earlier in MH1.
MH1–2 differ as follows: m.3, tenor, n.2 is a dotted sixteenth; m.4, treble, nn.1–3 slurred; tenor nn.2–4 slurred; m.5, tenor, nn.1–3 slurred.

Performance note: m.7, treble, tenor, the grace notes are appoggiaturas performed as quarter notes with the following dotted quarter notes performed as eighth notes.

PRETORIUM

No text att. Watts, *Hymns* II, No. 95, stanzas 1–6. The entire hymn is set. Text source differs as follows: m.53, "'Twere" instead of "'Twas;" m.66, "a" instead of "the;" m.68, "'Twere" instead of "'Twas."

MH2

MH2 differs as follows: m.57, all parts, quarter rest instead of eighth rest; m.75, all parts, quarter rest instead of eighth rest; m.76, treble, quarter rest instead of eighth rest; m.84 slow paced over m.83; mm. 84–85, treble, bass, marks of distinction lacking.

Performance note: mm. 2, 60, treble, m. 11, treble, tenor, the grace notes are appoggiatura performed as quarter notes with the following dotted quarter notes performed as eighth notes; mm. 84–85, all parts, the wedge-shaped signs are "Marks of Distinction" and are to be performed as accents, not staccato marks; m.95, tenor, the grace note is an appoggiatura performed as a quarter note with the following half note performed as a quarter note.

QUINCY

No text att. Watts Psalm 50ii, stanza 1. Text source differs as follows: m.11, "the" instead of "his."

MH2

MH2 differs as follows: m.9, counter, tenor, bass, n.1 lacks fermata; m.19, counter, tenor, bass, n.1 lacks fermata; m.22, counter, tenor, bass, n.1 lacks fermata.

RAMA

No text att. The source of the text is unlocated.

MH2

Performance note: m.6, treble, the grace note is an appoggiatura performed as a half note with the following whole performed as a half note; m.11, treble, the grace note is an appoggiatura performed as a half note with the following dotted half note performed as a quarter note.

RANDOLPH

No text att. Watts Psalm 148, stanza 1.

MH2

Performance note: m.8, tenor, the grace note is an appoggiatura performed as a quarter note with the following dotted quarter note performed as an eighth note; m.16, tenor, the grace note is an appoggiatura performed as a quarter note with the following half note performed as a quarter note.

RESIGNATION

No text att. A hymn by Samuel Wesley, Sr., stanzas 1 and 3. Text supplied from Wesley, *Collection*, Hymn No. 7. Because of Babcock's unusual text selection, no further stanzas have been supplied.

MH2 Published earlier in MH1.

Performance note: mm.14–15, all parts, the wedge-shaped signs are "Marks of Distinction" and are to be performed as accents, not staccato marks.

RESOLUTION

No text att. Watts Psalm 55, stanza 1.

MH2

MH2 differs as follows: m.15, tenor, bass, no first or second endings.

ROXBURY

No text att. The source of the text is unlocated.

PA2 Not printed by Babcock.

SABBATH

No text att. A hymn by Philip Doddridge, stanzas 1–2. Stanzas renumbered to reflect Babcock's choice of text. Text supplied from Belknap, Hymn No. 157. Doddridge's hymn contains five stanzas, one of which will not fit Babcock's music. Stanza 4, as follows, has been omitted:

No rude alarms, no raging foes,
To interrupt the long repose;
No midnight shade, no clouded sun,
To veil the bright eternal noon.

MH2

MH2 differs as follows: m.18 Piano placed over barline between m.18 and m.19.

SMYRNA

No text att. Watts, *Hymns* II, No. 50, stanzas 1–3. The remaining stanzas of Watt's hymn do not fit Babcock's music, thus no further stanzas are supplied.

MH2

MH2 differs as follows: m.2, tenor, bass, n.1 fermata lacking; m.4, tenor, bass, n.1 fermata lacking.

Performance note: m.12, treble, tenor, the grace notes are appoggiaturas performed as quarter notes with the following dotted quarter note performed as eighth notes.

SOLITUDE

No text att. Watts, *Horae*, "Love on a Cross and a Throne," stanza 2. Stanzas renumbered to reflect Babcock's choice of text.

CH Not printed by Babcock.

Performance note: m.5, counter, tenor, nn.4–5, major seconds appear to be intentional.

SONG FOR THE ANNIVERSARY OF ST. JOHN THE BAPTIST, JUNE 24, 5802 [I.E., 1802]

Alternative title in MH2 Preface: MASON SONG. Alternative title in MH2 Index: SONG FOR THE ANNIVERSARY OF ST. JOHN.

Text att.: Words by the Rev. Mr. Harris. Source of text is unlocated. The Rev. Mr. Harris is most likely Thaddeus Mason Harris and the poem was probably written specifically for Babcock to set to music for a local 1802 celebration of the anniversary of St. John. In the Preface of MH2 Babcock wrote, "At the request of a number of gentlemen of that Fraternity, he [Babcock] has published, at the end of this Work, the MASON SONG, which was composed by their particular desire, and for their use."—[ii]. Harris breaks the meter in stanzas 2–3. Stanza 2, line 5 and stanza 3, lines 2 and 4 each have 13 syllables. See performance notes, below, for a possible solution in each case.

MH2

MH2 differs as follows: m.8, tenor, bass, fermatas lacking; m.21, bass, n.1 dot lacking; m.27, tenor, bass, nn.4–5, marks of distinction lacking; m.29, tenor, bass, n.5 fermatas lacking; m.33, tenor, bass, nn.4–5 marks of distinction lacking.

Performance notes: mm.1–8 and 29–33, the "symphonies" are passages for unspecified instruments. The instruments should also play along with the voices when they are singing; m.12, all parts, sing two syllables on the sixteenth notes to make stanza 3 fit the music; m.20, all parts, sing two syllables on the sixteenth notes to make stanza 3 fit the music; mm. 20–23, bass, the lower part should be played rather than sung; m.25, all parts, make quarter note into two eighths to make stanza 2 fit the music; m.27, all parts, m.32, bass, and m.33, all parts, the wedge-shaped signs are "Marks of Distinction" and are to be performed as accents, not staccato marks.

SPRING

No text att. An anonymous hymn, stanza 1. Text supplied from Belknap, Hymn No. 119.

MH2

MH2 differs as follows: m.8, tenor, bass, no first or second endings.

SPRINGFIELD [I]

No text att. Wesley, *Hymns*, Hymn No. 21, stanza 4. Text source differs as follows: m.18, "convulsions" instead of "convulsion." Underlaid text differs as follows: m.19, "The" added to beginning of line. Because Babcock broke the poetic meter, the remaining stanzas of Wesley's hymn do not fit the music, thus no further stanzas are supplied.

SH Not printed by Babcock.

Performance Note: The dissonances caused by the counter part in mm.6, 9–10, 18, and 21 have been removed in the second version of the tune.

SPRINGFIELD [II]

No text att. Wesley, *Hymns*, Hymn No. 21, stanza 4. Text source differs as follows: m.18, "convulsions" instead of "convulsion." Underlaid text differs as follows: m.19, "The" added to beginning of line. Because Babcock broke the poetic meter, the remaining stanzas of Wesley's hymn do not fit the music, thus no further stanzas are supplied.

CH Not printed by Babcock.

STOW

No text att. Newton, *Olney* I, No. 7, stanza 2. Stanzas renumbered to reflect Babcock's choice of text.

MH2 Published earlier in MH1.

MH2 differs as follows: m.20, tenor, n.2 is a quarter note (corrected in errata).

STRATTON

No text att. *New Version*, Psalm 34, stanzas 3–4. Since *New Version* numbers stanzas according to biblical verses, stanzas have been renumbered according to poetic meter.

MH2

Performance note: mm.2–3, 5, 15, treble, tenor, the grace notes are appoggiaturas performed as quarter notes with the following dotted quarter notes performed as eighth notes; m.8, treble, the grace note is an appoggiatura performed as a quarter note with the following half note performed as a quarter note.

SUNDAY

No text att. *New Version*, Psalm 118, stanza 24 followed by stanza 19. Because of Babcock's unusual text selection, no further stanzas have been supplied.

MH2

MH2 differs as follows: m.19, tenor, bass, no first or second endings.

TRIUMPH

No text att. A hymn by Elizabeth Scott, stanza 3. Text supplied from Leavitt, *Seamen's*, Hymn No. 431. This is the final stanza in the hymn. Underlaid text differs as follows: m.5, "hosanna" instead of "hosannas;" m.7, "humbler" instead of "humble."

MH2

MH2 differs as follows: m.16, counter, tenor, and bass, no first or second endings.

TRURO

No text att. *New Version*, Psalm 149, stanzas 1–2. Text supplied from Belknap, Psalm No. 149.

MH2

VERNON

No text att. Watts, Psalm 45i, stanza 1. Text supplied from Belknap (1795), Psalm No. 45i.

MH2

MH2 differs as follows: m.10, treble, n.2 stem lacking; m.14, tenor, bass, no first or second endings.

VIENNA

No text att. *New Version*, Psalm 148, stanza 1. Since *New Version* numbers stanzas according to biblical verses, stanzas have been renumbered according to poetic meter.

MH2

MH2 differs as follows: m.19, counter, tenor, bass, no first or second endings.

WALTHAM

No text att. Watts, *Hymns* I, No. 137, stanzas 1–2. Stanzas renumbered to reflect Babcock's choice of text. Text supplied from Winchell, Hymn No. 226. Text source differs as follows:

m.14, "nor" instead of "or." Watts's hymn contains five stanzas, one of which will not fit Babcock's music. Stanza 5, as follows, has been omitted:

He dies! and in that dreadful night
Did all the pow'rs of hell destroy;
Rising, he brought our heav'n to light,
And took possession of the joy.

MH2

MH2 differs as follows: m.15, bass, n.2 is a quarter note (corrected in errata).

WARREN

No text att. A poem by Thomas Flatman, stanza 1. Text supplied from MacKenzie, *Selection*, Hymn No. 667. The remaining stanzas of Flatman's poem do not fit Babcock's music, thus no further stanzas are supplied.

CH Not printed by Babcock.

Performance note: m.24, treble, tenor, the chromatic clash appears to be intentional.

WATERTOWN

No text att. Newton, *Olney* I, No. 57, stanzas 5–7. These are the final stanzas in the hymn. Text source differs as follows: m.3, "husband" instead of "and my."

MH2 Published earlier in MH1.

MH1–2 differ as follows: m.30, bass, no first or second endings.

Performance note: mm.8–11, all parts, the wedge-shaped signs are "Marks of Distinction" and are to be performed as accents, not staccato marks.

WESTBOROUGH

No text att. Watts, *Hymns* II, No. 62, stanzas 1–2 and 5. Text supplied from Winchell, Hymn No. 563. Because of Babcock's unusual text selection, no further stanzas have been supplied.

CH Not printed by Babcock.

WESTON

Text att.: Dr. Watt's Lyric Poems. Watts, *Horae*, "Confession and Pardon," stanzas 7–8. Stanzas renumbered to reflect Babcock's choice of text. The 15th and 16th stanzas of Watt's poem do not fit Babcock's music, thus they are not supplied.

MH2 Published earlier in MH1.

WILMINGTON

No text att. Watts, *Hymns* I, No. 5, stanza 3. Stanzas renumbered to reflect Babcock's choice of text. Text source differs as follows: m.2, "who" instead of "that."

MH2

WRENTHAM

No text att. The source of the text is unlocated.

CH Not printed by Babcock.

Index of Tune Names

Index of First Lines

9780815324089